KU-451-291

THE HARVARD LECTURES

THE HARVARD LECTURES

ANNA FREUD

Edited and annotated by

Joseph Sandler

The Institute of Psycho-Analysis

London

Karnac Books

London 1992

First published in 1992 by
H. Karnac (Books) Ltd.
58 Gloucester Road
London SW7 4QY

Copyright © 1992 The Anna Freud Centre

All rights reserved. No part of this book may be reproduced,
in any form, by any process or technique,
without the prior written permission of the publisher.

British Library Cataloguing in Publication Data.
A catalogue record for this book is available from the British
Library.

ISBN 1 85575 030 9

Printed in Great Britain by BPCC Wheatons Ltd, Exeter

CONTENTS

PREFACE

Joseph Sandler

T hese lectures were given by Anna Freud at Harvard University in 1952. They were recorded on tape and later copied from reels to cassettes. Copies of the cassettes were provided by Dr Martin Berezin of Boston, and the transcriptions have been edited by me as lightly as possible. Although Miss Freud did not read her lectures and possibly did not even speak from notes, the transformation of her spoken words into written text has been possible without significant alteration of the content of her talks; as a consequence her very special style of presentation is evident throughout. Anna Freud had given one lecture, which was not recorded, providing a general background to the topic of the psychoanalytic view of development and its application to child care. However, the nine lectures that followed—introduced by Talcott Parsons, Chairman of the Department of Social Relations at Harvard— represent a complete work in their own right. As she put it in the third lecture: 'my assignment here is two-sided: on the one hand, it is to make you acquainted with the psychoanalytic theories concerning childhood; on the other hand, it is to point out to you where these theories are of immediate concern to people who deal with the upbringing of children—namely, the parents.'

As always, Anna Freud's formulations were extremely clear, and reading them will recall many memories for those of us who knew her. Certainly it brought back vivid memories for me of the introductory course she gave in her home in Maresfield Gardens to students training in the British Psycho-Analytical Society. Yet in one way they are very different. In these lectures Anna Freud has clearly decided to avoid theoretical complexities; indeed, at times she has presented her ideas with breathtaking simplification. She once remarked, in reference to something she had presented, 'I stopped before giving the details, because I felt that they might harm the clarity of the picture I wanted to give. . . . I really wanted to show certain things very clearly. And to do that one had to exclude many of the details.' This special style of presentation, with its avoidance of technicalities, certainly owed much to her early training as a teacher, to her confident familiarity with psychoanalytic thinking, and, above all, to her view of children and parents as real people, struggling with real internal and external problems. Anna Freud's approach, from the very beginning, has been a *developmental* one, and this developmental approach has been extremely enriching to psychoanalytic theory and practice, as well as to the practical problems of child care, which she approaches psychoanalytically in these lectures. Anna Freud's writings show her great love for children and her concern for the problems of parents and caregivers. They also show the down-to-earth uncommon sense that is characteristic of all her work.

Although the ideas in these lectures are very simply presented, it is evident, if we read them from the perspective of her later work, how much she anticipated further developments in psychoanalysis. At the same time the lectures show the extent to which advances have been made in the viewpoint of developmental psychoanalysis during the last few decades. While there is no doubt that Anna Freud's lectures bear the stamp of their time, they serve the dual function of providing a most useful introduction to the psychoanalytic view of development and its application to child care, as well as giving us a most valuable historical document.

It gives me great pleasure to acknowledge the generosity of Martin Berezin, who provided the tapes from which the lectures were transcribed, the skill of Barbara Sullivan, who did the transcription, and the generosity of the Edith Ludowyk-Gyomroi Trust, which funded some of the transcription costs. I want to take the opportunity to express my appreciation to the late George Moran, Director of the Anna Freud Centre and Editor of its Bulletin (in which the lectures were first published), for his help and encouragement. His tragic death this month robbed child psychoanalysis of an outstanding scholar, clinician, researcher and administrator.

London
January 1992

THE HARVARD LECTURES

Introduction

Talcott Parsons

I n 1950, Anna Freud, the daughter of Sigmund Freud, a person—as those who know her are well aware— distinguished in her own right, first visited the United States to receive an honorary degree at Clark University. On that occasion Radcliffe College and the Department of Social Relations at Harvard were fortunate in being able to sponsor a public lecture by Miss Freud on some of the implications of psychoanalytic theory for the care of children, which has been her special field. This was delivered to an audience consisting largely of Harvard and Radcliffe undergraduates, and the enthusiasm of her reception was so great that President Jordan and I, very soon after this occasion, began discussing the possibility of bringing Miss Freud to Harvard and Radcliffe for a more extended visit, when students would have an opportunity to hear her lectures on psychoanalytic theory at greater length.

This did not become possible until the early fall of 1952, when it was arranged for Miss Freud to come here for a four-week period. This was under the auspices of Radcliffe College, the Department of Social Relations and the Laboratory of

1

Human Development in the Faculty of Education. The course which you are about to hear was one of three major obligations which Miss Freud undertook during her visit here. This was specifically meant for undergraduates and was a course on the psychoanalytic theory of child development. It was limited to one hundred participants so that it would not be unduly large, but was also merged with the course on the development of the child ordinarily given and carried on the rest of the term by Professor Sears. Therefore she lectured three times a week to a group normally of about two hundred students. You will judge for yourselves about the content of this course. You might, however, be interested that in addition to this Miss Freud served as a consultant to the research staff of the Laboratory of Human Development, which has for several years been carrying on intensive research in what is essentially her field. Finally, specifically for the Department of Social Relations, she conducted a seminar for members of the faculty staff on more advanced problems of psychoanalytic theory, this time without special reference to child development. This seminar provided an opportunity for the staff to engage in very fruitful discussions of theoretical problems which are of the greatest interest to all aspects of social relations. Needless to say, all three of the sponsoring agencies were greatly honoured to be able to have Miss Freud with us for this four-week period and hope that it may be repeated at some time in the future.

Since the first of Miss Freud's lectures was not recorded, I am glad to be able to give you a very brief resumé of the subject-matter she covered at that time. In her first lecture Miss Freud introduced the subject of the development of the child from the psychoanalytic standpoint and described the child as having great potentialities for growth. In making this approach she did not minimize the influence of the mother's care on the developing personality. On the contrary, she emphasized the intimate relationship between those properties of the child with which he was endowed at birth and the nurturing influences of his family experiences. Miss Freud discussed the importance of the child's motivational development for the future tasks of learning in school, adjusting to the needs of other persons and developing a stable and effective pattern of life for himself.

This introductory lecture was designed by Miss Freud to present a general framework within which to develop her subsequent theories. It was with the next lecture, with which the present recordings begin, that Miss Freud began her technical presentation of the principles of personality development as viewed through the data and methods of psychoanalysis.

The unconscious

I am looking for remarks, queries, or criticisms in the written comments that have been given to me, but all I have is what I picked up by chance since the last time I spoke. I have learnt a few interesting facts. For one thing, there are no blank minds here—everybody present has heard about psychoanalysis before. There seem to be no people either, from what I have heard, who need to have their prejudices against psychoanalytic theory destroyed. Either there are no prejudices, or the people with them have not come. So all that is left in the audience are the knowledgeable ones, and they are just those at whom I had not aimed what I had to say last time. I'm afraid I did actually disappoint or bore some people by being what you might consider to be too simple. But there I would like you to take two points into account. We only created a frame last time to put in our facts, but a frame can be very simple indeed, and the picture inside can be very complicated. Also, you have to get used to the fact that I use very simple language, which does not mean always that the facts are easy and not complex.

I do not know whether there are people here who were not here last time, but if there are, I would just like to summarize what I said in two sentences. We had committed ourselves last time to a particular entrance into the psychoanalytic views on childhood development—namely, an entrance from the side of the upbringing of the child—and we characterized education or upbringing as the help or the push given to the child towards adaptation to society. And we found that there are two ways of inducing the child to take that step: one, by making him conform, whatever his nature; the other, by inducing him to change his nature. There is a third way, which is not to be recommended, and which I hope none of you will follow, which is to try to change the environment of the child so that it fits the nature of the child. That is all wrong. It does not work out well for the child, and for the adult community it means a loss in cultural values. It is the child who should go forward into the community.

Well, by taking that approach we have adopted at the same time what one might call a non-objective attitude towards the study of personality—that is, we have committed ourselves to look at the various parts of the developing child's personality from a particular point of view, from a point of view of whether this or that particular part fits into the adult community. We ask how far it is susceptible to influence from the environment, what the influences may be, how far this particular part of the child's personality is modifiable, what the modifications are, and what are the forces that bring about the modification. That is the approach that we have to take now.

The knowledgeable among you have certainly recognized the three parts, or the three aspects of the personality which I mentioned last time—namely the instinctive aspect,[1] the rational aspect, and the moral aspect. These are the three well-known parts of the personality, called in psychoanalytic theory the id, ego, and superego. For those who do not feel quite com-

---

[1]Throughout these Lectures, Anna Freud uses the term 'instinctive' where we would now use 'instinctual', retaining 'instinctive' for the type of 'given' behaviour described by ethologists.

fortable with these three terms or concepts, I would like to make a few warning remarks. Though the terms correspond to what we find in a dissection of the personality—to what in the literature has actually been called the 'anatomy' of the human personality, they should by no means be considered in an anatomical sense. They have nothing to do with the brain. You won't find the id in one part of the brain, the ego in another, and the superego somewhere else. Attempts at making some correlation between brain anatomy and these divisions within the personality were made long ago—sixty years ago—and failed then. It is quite recently that, here or there, brain neurologists interested in analysis or analysts who know something about brain neurology have again, after a lapse of sixty years, taken up attempts of this kind. I don't know whether you have heard of certain brain operations[2] which are being performed on very ill psychotic patients in the attempt to put certain parts of their personality out of action. There are some enthusiastic people in that field who actually believe that such a correlation between anatomy and psychoanalysis can be found. But it is certainly not what I am trying to present to you. So please think of id, ego, and superego as quite unrelated to space, as merely abstractions, just as we, in ordinary language, talk about 'parts' of ourselves—one part of myself wanted to do this, and in another part of myself I didn't want to—without actually drawing lines in the body indicating that this part wanted it and that part didn't. It is not meant that way at all. But it is also not meant in another way that has often bothered people. There are many scientifically minded people who have objected to the personification of the parts of the human personality. I remember somebody calling the id, ego, and superego the three mythical personalities—a sort of holy Trinity. It is not meant that way either. These terms are meant to designate groups of functions (I see you are writing that down—I always notice when I say something that seems important!). All the functions grouped together serve identical purposes; that is why we group them together. To

---

[2]Anna Freud referred here to prefrontal leucotomy or to lobotomy.

give you an example, that part of the personality which we put together under the name of id, the instinctive part of the personality, serves the purposes of the instincts; and whatever serves the purposes of the instincts in that way, and is concerned with the instincts,[3] belongs to that part, to the id.

Again, the group of functions called the ego has a common purpose—namely, to maintain the individuals in their environment, which means learning to know the environment, to form some link between what goes on in the depths of the person (in the id) and in the outside world, and to bring the two into some sort of contact. We group together as the ego the part of the personality charged with the functions serving that purpose. It is really the self-preservation of the individual that you find there.

And then there is the third group, which serves so-called cultural purposes: the superego, with the function of conscience and moral assessment of actions undertaken or thoughts that go on in the person. This group of functions— the superego functions—serve the purpose of maintaining the individual as a member of the community.

So try, in what follows now, to think of these three parts of the human being as three functional groups, and let us now, in the whole of the course that follows, trace the development of these three parts, examine in detail how they fulfil their purposes, at what time they appear in the child's life, and, most important, how they react towards each other. Their hostile reactions towards each other you will meet under the heading of 'conflict'—internal conflict.

Well, that is the task. And let us begin at that end of the personality which is furthest removed from the external world

---

[3]In the early translations of Freud, the German term *Trieb* was rendered in English as 'instinct'; this is a misleading translation, and *Trieb* would nowadays be translated as 'drive'. Nevertheless the use of the term 'instinct' for *Trieb* has tended to remain, although in much of the English-language psychoanalytic literature the term 'instinctual drive' is used.

and even further removed from the cultural aims—namely, the id. So this is our hour for id psychology.

There is one very important point to remember about the id. It does not connect with the environment; worse than that, it is not in direct connection with the other parts of the personality—at least not in visible connection. Every individual may be ignorant of the largest part of this id group of functions within himself; and since the id is not accessible to consciousness, we say that the content of the id is to a large degree unconscious.

Now we have arrived at something which everybody knows. It is a very curious fact that the psychology of the unconscious, the postulation of an unconscious mind which we now call the id, once the most controversial point about the whole of psychoanalytic theory, has, with time, become the most familiar idea to us.[4] In the early years of psychoanalysis, for instance, a course of lectures of this kind (the audience would not have been so large) would have been taken up wholly with justifying the existence of an unconscious part of the mind. Nowadays, if one talks to audiences about psychoanalysis, one has to be very careful not to underestimate their knowledge in this respect, because so much of it is not only taught in many other disciplines but has actually reached large parts of the population. It has become common knowledge; talk about it has become common usage. Therefore I thought I would be wise to separate in these lectures two parts of the psychology of the unconscious, or the id—one part which I assume is known to you and I need only remind you of it, and another part where I have the feeling that even if it is not new you are less familiar with it.

And now for the first half first. What do I think that you know about the unconscious, or the id? I hope you will correct me afterwards if I have grouped it wrong, it would be very interesting for me. I think you are all convinced of the existence of the unconscious mind. You do not receive that curious shock

---

[4]Anna Freud, clearly for purposes of exposition, makes an enormous conceptual simplification here in equating the unconscious mind with the id. She clarifies this point in lecture two.

any more, you don't feel offended in the same manner as in the past by the fact that you do not know everything about yourself, about your own emotions; and as scientists, as psychologists, you are certainly much less inclined to assert that the psychological, the mental, and the conscious are identical, an assertion made for hundreds of years. I think you would all agree now that the psychological extends far beyond the conscious, and that we have to widen consciousness carefully and gradually to learn something about the real limits of our mind. The limits of consciousness are very narrow.

I think there is another point very well known to everybody. There was a time when people began to concede the existence of an unconscious mind, when they got used to the idea, but somehow found it very difficult to imagine that an idea, an inner structure or an inner movement, of which we know nothing, could have any force; whereas, as you know, the psychoanalytic assertion is that the unconscious is dynamic, full of forces, that it is really the reservoir of forces in us. When we make a certain idea conscious, far from it increasing in strength, its strength decreases, as if part of its energy has been let out in the action of becoming conscious. The more unconscious an idea, a certain constellation, is in us, the stronger it is. People used to think that the idea of strong unconscious forces is not a nice feeling to have about oneself, because one never knows what one will be moved by in the next moment. But we are used to that idea now, you all are. I am quite sure you would not make the mistake, if anyone asks you for the motivation for your actions, of asserting that you know all about it, that you know exactly why you have chosen the area of study or the profession in which you find yourself, that you know exactly why you like certain people and dislike others, or why you choose your partners. People used to think they knew all about such things, and now we all know that the most important steps in our life are taken because we are driven from inside to take them; but really we are all the more eager to carry out a certain action the less we know the motive for it—this is still felt to be not a very nice idea. But when you find somebody set absolutely intently on a certain course, and when you find that no amount of reasoning will put him off it, you can be quite certain that he is motivated not for reasons that he knows but by causes that he does not know. And, as I said before, it is a fact that the most important decisions in life are taken on the basis of unconscious motivation.

Well, if you are familiar with that idea you probably are also familiar with an interesting addition to it—namely, that we are seldom caught out appearing not to know about our motives. That is to say, if we are asked why we do something we can always give an answer. But when somebody else studies us in that particular situation, or analyses us, then it is easy to prove that the answer that we have given is one that has been invented quickly for the purpose, that it is merely brought forward by consciousness to hide the fact that the real motivation is unknown to us. Such apparently reasonable motivation, which really covers over our unconscious motivation, is called 'rationalization': it sounds rational, but it isn't. Those of you who have read more about the subject will probably remember where this rationalization was discovered first. I know there are some people here interested in hypnosis—I spoke to one of them the other day—and it was actually with people under hypnosis that this rationalization was discovered first. Under hypnosis they were given certain suggestions to carry out an action and were then told to forget all about it. When they actually carried it out, they had very good reasons for it, but not the real reasons. This rationalization is a very interesting and widespread business!

Well, now the more familiar facts about the unconscious. People find it very difficult to imagine that the unconscious is *really* unconscious. You know, in scientific writings, too, people have made all sorts of attempts to show that the unconscious is just that little bit less conscious, it's a sort of shady consciousness, it's something at the borders of consciousness, it's subconscious. All that is not the meaning in our psychoanalytic theory. The meaning is quite plain, as I said, that the person knows nothing about it. People have tried to invent all sorts of tricks to, one could say, surprise the unconscious, to draw it into consciousness. It's been suggested that if one hypnotized a person and let him talk under hypnosis, in that way we'd reach the unconscious; and that if we put what we heard on a tape recorder and played it back to the person, then he would know it was his unconscious. But he would not. People try with drugs to lower the resistances, as we would call it, to surprise the unconscious by telling what has been found, giving it back to the person in the experiment; but the person does not recognize his own unconscious. You should believe in all earnest, even if so far you have only heard it talked about or talked about it, that it needs an enormous effort from the side of the conscious mind to reach what is unconscious, and that effort and good will alone do not do it. You have to use certain methods, and the psychoanalytic technique is one of these methods. The reason is that there is a barrier between the id and the other parts of the personality, and that barrier prohibits the inhabitants (I now speak in personifications) of the one realm from entering the other, and where some part of that realm wants to enter, it has to overcome what we call a resistance—which is a very strong force.

You have heard about this difficulty in reaching the unconscious, but equally you have heard of that quality or tendency of the unconscious to break through suddenly and surprise us. For instance, you know that our moods come from the unconscious. We don't know why we suddenly feel happy or dejected, or why we wake up in a certain state of mind, and perhaps change completely during the day. As I said before, we know very little where our likes and dislikes come from. There are people who are subject to outbreaks of temper which they cannot control: these are unconscious forces coming up. There are severe outbreaks of passions which should remain well within the unconscious, which lead people to crimes—crimes of violence, for instance; and there are the illnesses such as psychotic outbreaks where this barrier between conscious and unconscious, ego and id, gives way altogether. So on the one hand we have a strict control of traffic between the two parts of the personality, and on the other hand, we have sudden inroads from the unconscious.

Well, I assume you have known all that, and I think that even if you had not known it in the way I have told it, you have met all these facts individually. Now I would like to go over further ground and enquire into single points, and you can see whether your knowledge has gone deep enough and wide enough. For instance, when you talk about the unconscious or the id, are you really aware of the fact that in psychoanalytic terminology this is the concept which covers the sum total of a person's instinctive life? (I use the term 'instinct' here, which I hope you will understand in the analytic sense; it is a term we use for instinctive drives or instinctive urges, wishes, desires). Instinctive life, which means those drives that come from the body and become represented somehow in the individual's mind, are felt in the mind as a claim. This is because every instinctive urge of this kind, whether it is a sexual wish or an aggressive wish, or any of the wishes that belong to one of these two groups, creates an enormous tension in the personality; and the conscious part of the personality feels that tension. There is no peace until that tension is reduced, and it is reduced when that particular instinctive urge reaches its aim and finds satisfaction—as, for instance, when a particular aggressive drive finds an outlet against the person against whom it is directed, or when a particular sexual wish can satisfy itself on the person towards whom it is directed. What happens is very much according to the pattern of the great body-needs where the tension created by hunger is only satisfied when food is taken in. What we visualize as the id part of the human personality is the realm where all this happens, where the pressure of the drives is felt and where action is undertaken to satisfy the drives. We will spend a good deal of time later learning more about the various types of drives. At the moment I only want to mention that we recognize two big groups, what you might call the constructive and the destructive ones, represented in the mind by sex on the one hand, and destruction–aggression on the other hand. The principle according to which this functions in the id is a very simple one: the human organism strives for peace, and peace means getting rid of tension. So wherever tension from a drive arises, a move is made towards finding satisfaction. I am quite certain that you have often dealt with this particular theory under the title of 'wish fulfilment', and it is a very good idea to think of functioning according to the principle of wish fulfilment, not as a petty fulfilling of small daily conscious wishes but as the overall attempt on the part of the id-organization to satisfy every drive as it arises. That's a tall order, of course, for what the id would like to do is to satisfy every drive as it arises and to return to a tensionless state which is felt as pleasurable. Again, you may recognize an old acquaintance here—namely, the idea that functioning in the primitive personality occurs according to the pleasure–pain principle. This means merely that whole realm of the unconscious is only concerned with trying to avoid painful tension and gaining pleasurable satisfaction—something that is quite far removed from the way we all actually live.

There is another point that usually does not find enough consideration. I mean that it is a main characteristic of the id that it pursues this policy of wish fulfilment at any price, completely regardless of what happens in the environment; regardless of the fact that the fulfilment, let us say, of an aggressive drive hurts somebody else, and regardless of the fact that the fulfilment of a wish can hurt the individual himself. So we say that this type of functioning is completely blind, blind towards reality, orientated only towards the drives and their gratification. Now you will soon get an actual picture of the primitivity or, as one might say, the crudity of id functioning.

There are two smaller points that are often disregarded. When people talk of id, ego, and superego and are aware of what has to happen in an analytic treatment, they usually regard the unconscious as a small addition to the conscious personality. For instance, somebody may be bothered by symptoms of some kind, look for relief in treatment, and come to the analyst with the idea that there is a little bit of something in his unconscious that he would like to get rid of. You can actually hear quite serious people ask in analysis whether there is still much more to come, or whether the end of their unconscious has been reached. In former times, when knowledge was less and prejudices were stronger, many people used to be afraid of psychoanalytic treatment, having the idea that their unconscious would be 'analysed out', and nothing would be left. I remember very well people asking me in former years whether well-analysed people (which they hoped I was) still had feelings—I mean this quite seriously! They would ask whether their emotions were not now all conscious and clear, whether anything was really left in the background. This shows such an enormous misunderstanding, a misconception of the relative size of the two agencies in the mind. I mean the basic personality, which is the id, and then what is put on top of it, the ego that is developed out of it—that we will hear about next time— is comparatively very small in size, very powerless as far as energy is concerned.[5] Isn't it curious, then, that when we talk of ourselves, when we say 'I', we mean the conscious part? I suppose it can be explained by the fact that the unconscious, the id, somehow does not belong to us in the same sense, it is not personal. It is very much the same in everybody, it is what we bring into the world, what is inborn, what we share with everybody else; whereas our own personal individual qualities are developed out of it very gradually in the ego and superego. But as far as force and relative space is concerned—if we can use the word 'space' for something that is spaceless—well, the id has it, there's no doubt about it.

The whole thing becomes even more interesting when we realize that what happens within the id is so completely different from what happens in the conscious parts of our personality. The id has a special way of functioning. I have mentioned that it follows a special principle, that it is completely regulated by the pleasure–pain principle, by the need to reduce tension, to avoid the unpleasurable. But in this we see that the id is organized completely differently from the conscious part of the mind. Again, as you know, in psychoanalysis one has gained some insight into that different mode of functioning through the study of dreams, where the id reveals itself, and through the study of those mental illnesses where the id, even though it does not appear completely, of course, reveals itself to a certain extent. It took many years—forty or fifty—to put together these inklings of the modes of functioning within the id. I will give you

---

[5]There is increasing realization that the ego, regarded as a structure, has powerful unconscious roots and functions, which develop autonomously. Anna Freud's formulation in this context is clearly intended to counter the tendency to underestimate the force of the drives and the degree to which they are unconscious. The same device is used in the equation of 'ego' with 'self' or with consciousness.

a few examples that may interest you. For instance, we feel in our conscious personality that we are one, and we actually are one (we are if we leave out the division of our minds into three), but so far as we actually consciously know, we are more or less unified. I mean, for instance, that if we love somebody, we don't usually hate him at the same time—the two don't go together. But when we feel the two feelings in us they mix and reduce each other. If we have two wishes, the two wishes come together and are integrated in some way. If we pursue a purpose, we reduce other purposes for the sake of purpose number one. That is so natural to us that we never think about it. But sometimes you can hear the curious remarks of people who say, 'Well, I feel all torn to pieces, I don't know whether I'm here or there. Do I want to do this or that?' when suddenly for a moment this feeling of integration of purpose is absent. But in the id there is nothing of the kind. As I said to you before, the id is full of wishes, urges, desires, but they don't touch each other. They pursue the most opposite aims immediately, one after another or even simultaneously. The one has nothing to do with the other. We see that in dreams.[6]

There is another possibility of seeing how the id operates, not in pure culture but approximately. When you study children between one and two years of age, when id functioning still plays a great part even though the ego is fully in the process of development, you can surprise some of these id modes of functioning. For instance, a child will hit mother one moment and love her the next, and not feel guilty for the hitting. The child does not feel that the hitting and the loving don't go together. What we see is just the expression of two tendencies. Or the child will break a toy and expect it to be whole the next moment, because one wish in the child wants to break the toy and the other wish wants the whole toy; but the two have nothing to do with each other. The examples are endless. What is

---

[6]Dreams do, of course, show a substantial degree of integration and compromise formation. What is meant here is that the opposing impulses in the id or their derivatives in the dream can be discerned in analysis.

meant is there is no integration within the id, it is a mass, a heap, with no communication between the single parts of it—something that is absolutely alien to our conscious mode of functioning. We call that function—we will hear next time about when it actually begins in the human being—'synthesis' or 'ego integration'.

Well, you know, thinking or imagining goes on quite differently in the id and in the ego. We think in words, and even if we have fantasies and dreams, fantasies are altogether in words[7] and dreams are partly so, accompanied by images. But in the id there are no words; instincts have no words, they create imaginings, pictures. For instance, the hungry baby will imagine the food, the milk; or the lonely baby will imagine the mother coming; but he will not be able to think, 'I want my mother', or to express it that way. The whole imagery in our dreams is a sign of the language of the id, of the unconscious. It is, of course, very difficult for us to imagine a form of expression in which words are absent, where everything has to be expressed in images. It means that ever so many things cannot be expressed at all. For instance, logical connections or the correlation between ideas cannot be expressed without words—but there are no logical connections in the id, and there are no correlations of this kind. There is hardly a before and an after. There is certainly no 'because' or 'since'. The language of the unconscious is very much like hieroglyphics. For students of the unconscious it is a very good exercise to try, for instance, to read a short article and then to try to reproduce it without words, just in pictures that are drawn. We will find that it can't be done in any way that will satisfy our consciousness. For instance, there is in the unconscious nothing like a negation. Let us say that the child would want to express the idea, 'I am afraid of birds', in a dream. So a bird would appear in the dream; but if we read the dream script, we

---

[7]This is clearly an oversimplification. Daydream fantasies and nighttime dreams differ in important respects, but both involve images as well as words. Nevertheless, the distinction made here between 'id' and 'ego' is of supreme importance.

would not know whether it meant 'I want to have a bird' or 'I
never want to have a bird' or 'there was no bird' or 'I hadn't
seen one': the positive and the negative are expressed in quite
the same way. That is the language of the unconscious, that is
why it is so difficult to understand, and that is why analysts
have to do so much guess-work. We try to translate the language of the unconscious into that of consciousness.

There are more things that are not present in that primitive
mode of functioning. So there is no sense of time, and the
content of the unconscious does not become old. For example,
a wish—let us say, to have the mother for one's own—can stay
alive in the unconscious from the time the child is six months
old until the same person is an adult of forty or fifty or sixty.
The wishes do not change, do not get weaker, only change
according to one principle—namely, that there is an inborn
sequence of instinctive wishes not influenced from the side of
the environment. We will talk about that another time when we
talk about the contents of the unconscious.

There is another curious thing which makes the unconscious seem very strange to us. There is a very easy displacement of energy. For instance, sexual energy attached to one
image may flow over to another image. This flowing-over is very
easy. I remember the story of a child who had a lot of difficulty
owing to her unconscious fears. Her mode of expression
showed quite a bit of unconscious functioning. She was very
angry with her doctor because she was terribly afraid of doctors
(she was a very little girl). She met her doctor on the street and
said to her, 'I'll kill you', and the doctor said, 'I thought you
liked me', and she said, 'All right, I'll kill another doctor', which
means there was an easy displacement; energy and image are
not as closely connected in the id as are the ties that are formed
later on by our forms of logical thinking.

Well, I have given you a very quick overall picture—on the
one hand, of the principle of functioning in the id, on the other
of the mode of functioning, because I wanted you to understand
two things: on the one hand, how very necessary the barrier is
which divides this life of the id from our ordinary life—actually
the normality of our behaviour in daily life depends on the id
not invading the other parts of our personality. And, on the

other hand, I wanted you to understand that due to that barrier—coming back now to our orientation, to psychoanalytic theory, so far as it is important for the use of parents—well, this shows you that the parents have no influence on the id of the child. The id of the child, as I have described it to you now, is removed from the environment, does not care for the environment in that respect, and is not influenced by it, except in one point. The parents have one power over the child. The child is unable, in the early stages, to get instinct gratification for himself, but since he is under the powerful need of reducing tension and getting pleasure from instinct fulfilment, he is dependent on the parents. The parents can give satisfaction or withhold it. And indirectly, through creating a fate for the instinct, a pleasurable or unpleasurable one, they influence the child's id—or, rather, they have a connection with it; but not otherwise.

Well, that is the result of today's attempt to present you with the psychology of the unconscious, and the idea is that next time we take the next step and see how out of that unconscious base of the personality develops what we gradually call the human being.

Ego and id

The flow of questions has begun. I hope it will continue, because it is a great help in keeping me straight on course and nearer to responding to your wishes. Those who sent in questions should not be disappointed if I do not always answer them straight away. Most of the questions are very good, very justified, and bring up excellent material—but they belong in later regions of our course. So I don't want to interrupt the connections in what I have to say to answer them but will pay special attention to them when we have reached the places where they belong.

There is an immediate question, which concerns the material we discussed last time. I think I worried several people by apparently equating the id and the unconscious, and several questions have been sent up, asking whether I really meant to do that. I find it quite easy to identify myself with the bewilderment of the people who ask the questions, because they must wonder whether I have never heard about the changes that have taken place in that connection in the last twenty-six years. One does not equate the unconscious and the id in newer theory.[1] You may well ask whether I know that one can use the word 'unconscious' in various senses, and in what sense I have used it. Probably the people who asked this were referring to the double usage of unconscious: on the one hand, the descriptive sense and on the other the dynamic sense. Descriptively speaking, whatever is not in our conscious mind and within our awareness at a certain moment is unconscious. But that does not mean that it cannot become conscious the next moment, since our conscious mind only has room for a certain number of thoughts and images at any given time. In the descriptive sense, then, what is present in our mind at a given moment is conscious; what is not present there is unconscious. That is pure description, and it does not take us very far. But there is also a dynamic sense of the word, in which we use the term 'unconscious' for those thoughts and images that are not capable of becoming conscious without overcoming a considerable counterforce, as I pointed out last time. That is the unconscious of which I talked in the last lecture. It is unconscious, and it cannot easily become conscious. But, in addition to this, the term 'unconscious' was in use in earlier times in a third sense, in the systemic sense, designating one whole region of the mind, the system Unconscious, approximately the same as that which we now call the id. That sense has gone out of use.[2] and that is where I confused you last time—it was not that I had forgotten, but I wanted to avoid some of the complications of our

---

[1]Here Anna Freud rectifies a simplification she had made in the lecture one. The reference to 'the last twenty-six years' is to Freud's 1926 book, *Inhibitions, Symptoms and Anxiety* (1926d [1925], *Standard Edition, 20*), in which he introduced some radical revisions in psychoanalytic theory.

[2]This is a reference to the system Unconscious of the 'topographical' model of the mind, put forward by Freud in 1900 in *The Interpretation of Dreams* (1900a, *Standard Edition, 4 & 5*) in which the mind was conceived of as being divided into the regions Unconscious, Preconscious, and Perceptual-Conscious. This model was replaced in 1923 in *The Ego and The Id,* (1923b, *Standard Edition, 19*), with its concepts of id, ego and superego. However, for many purposes the original topographical formulations are still useful.

theory (you have no idea how many complications I spare you as I go along). Well, we can't use the word 'unconscious' for a part of the mind any more, because our mind is not divided up in an orderly way. It is not so that whatever belongs to the id, even in a remote way, is unconscious, whereas whatever belongs to the ego or superego is conscious. All the derivatives and representatives of the id can reach consciousness; and a great deal of the ego's functioning goes on without being accompanied by consciousness. A large part of the content of the ego is not conscious, and large parts of the superego are not conscious at all. So instead of dividing the mind into a system of 'the unconscious' and a system of 'consciousness' we are now dividing it into id, ego, and superego, in which the quality of consciousness or unconsciousness varies. Last time I represented to you that aspect of the id which is unconscious, and that's why I used the term in the way I did. I hope I have answered the questions of the people who were worried about this.

There were further questions, and they showed me quite clearly the points where the last lecture made you feel a bit uncomfortable. The question arose in the minds of many whether it is really true that the id is a closed system without communication with the outside world. Can such a thing be? And can such an organism exist? And you were quite right to be worried. Such a thing cannot be, and such an organism cannot exist—and besides, I did not say there is no communication between the id and the environment. I said something slightly different. I said that functioning in the id takes no notice of the environment, that the id functions according to its own principle which is strictly one of wish fulfilment: fulfilment of instinct satisfaction no matter what happens in the outside world. I also said the id has no organ of perception, no instrument to take notice of the outside world, by which I meant not until it develops one. The id would, indeed, be a closed system if it were not open towards the environment in one place— namely, where the fulfilment of the id-needs of the drives is located. If we were to think of a satisfied id where every need is fulfilled as it arises, then we would have a closed system. But such a thing happens perhaps in one situation only—that is, in the unborn child, in the foetus carried inside the mother, with all its needs automatically fulfilled through the agency of the mother's body. From the moment of birth onward there are needs that have to be fulfilled, and for these needs the environment is necessary.

You may remember another remark I made last time, that the contact with the environment is the one chance which the environment—for instance, the parents—has to get some indirect influence over the drives of the child, although the parents can have no direct influence. They can control the drives to a certain extent by giving or by withholding satisfaction. The child, once born, needs the fulfilment of its wishes, and since it does not yet have the possibility of controlling, changing, or of dealing with the environment, one adult person at least—the mother or her substitute—is necessary to keep that young organism alive. This means that the mother fulfils the function of being the link between the child's needs and the environment, until something happens in the development of the child which helps the young individual to take over that role himself. So perhaps that answers the question about whether or not the id is a closed system.

I think I warned you that you would have to take what I say here from a particular aspect—do you remember that I used the word 'anatomy'? What I am trying to give you here, though it has nothing to do with the brain or the body, might in some way be called the anatomy of the human personality. Well, what I do is to present you with sections of it, and naturally each section by itself makes no sense. If you were at an anatomical lecture and were demonstrated a stomach all by itself, you would say, 'this cannot exist, this needs a mouth, this needs some communication with the food outside, something to lead from the mouth to the interior or the stomach. How else should the food arrive?' They cannot function by themselves—but for the purpose of studying them, learning about them, analysing them, we have to take them piecemeal. So you had the id last time just as a piece of the personality, and we are now trying to link it up again with the other pieces that transform one segment into the beginning of a growing organism.

The id, then, has to create its link with the environment. This link, which is gradually created by modifying part of the original chaotic structure I described to you last time, will then be what we call the 'ego'. I will try to show you gradually how this ego is built up. Again I look for guidance to a question someone posed at the end of the last lecture—that if everything is unconscious in the id, what about the sensations that arise? Well, that's just it. What is unconscious are the drives themselves. What comes to the awareness of the individual are the sensations, the 'tensions' as I called them last time, which are felt as unpleasure or pain when they are raised, as pleasure when they are lowered through the instincts being given satisfaction. This means that what the newborn infant is aware of is a range of sensations from inside—sensations of pleasure and pain which guide the id's functioning, which always goes towards the gaining of pleasure and the avoidance of pain. That is all the awareness we have at first. But then we immediately have a second group of sensations or perceptions which come to the awareness of the infant. They are the perceptions which are derived from the sense organs, the sensations of hot and cold and wet and dry, the sensations from the skin that are derived from the child's body being touched by the mother or by the material that envelops the child, and so on; they are noises, they are the sensations of light; some of them are pleasurable; but above a certain intensity they are always painful to the child. The child's awareness, then, is full of these two lines of sensation, arising from inside and from outside. The first nucleus of what later will come to be called the ego is formed around these sensations, around the pleasurable and the painful sensations that we imagine as collected in what we might call a centre of awareness, the nucleus of the ego.

In the very beginning the child does not distinguish between what arrives from outside and what arrives from inside. That is, as you know, a well-known fact. A stomach-ache which sends up very painful sensations to the child's awareness is in no way distinguished or is in no way different for the child from, let us say, a loud noise which creates a painful acoustic sensation. The first function the child develops in this respect—we might say the first important ego function—is a distinction between sensations from inside and perceptions from outside; the term we use for that in psychoanalysis is that

child has learned to 'test reality'. It takes several months before this testing of reality is perfected by the child. I can give
you some very simple examples of how this function develops.
A hungry child has painful sensations coming from his
stomach, but since that child has already had experiences of
satisfaction which are connected with the appearance of the
mother, with the mother's breast, or with the bottle of milk, he
calls up alongside the pain of hunger the image of the satisfying object in the outer world. The satisfying object might be, as
I said, the bottle, the milk, the breast, the mother. It concerns
the child only so far as it is satisfying. This calling up of the
image of the satisfying object is an inner image and does not
satisfy the child; but if the same image appears in reality in the
person of the mother, in the reality of the bottle and the milk, it
may look the same to the child, yet it is a perception arising
from outside. These two events, the inner and the outer, are
only distinguished from each other by the experience of satisfaction that follows the outer one, the real one, but not the
inner. The distinction between the two guides the child to a
knowledge of—to a distinction between—outer reality and an
internal world of images. I don't know whether that sounds
very complicated to you, but it may help if you to remember
that later in life, when we have no difficulty any more in distin-
guishing between the productions of our own imagination and
the real pictures coming from the outside world, we still
have moments when we fall back into the infant state. In our
dreams we have very vivid pictures of the outside world, but
they only bring us the semblance of satisfaction. We wake up
unsatisfied. In the simplest forms of dream, the hunger dream
where we dream of food, the experience is very nice while we
dream, but we are just as hungry when we wake up, whereas
the same picture offered to us by the outside world comes from
the satisfying food. We know that at the height of the activity of
our imagination it can happen that sometimes we confuse a
very satisfactory fantasy structure with reality, but we do this
only for a short moment. But there are mental illnesses where
people actually return to the state of the infant, where they
have hallucinations, which means that they mistake the productions of their own inner wishful thinking for appearances

and experiences in the outside world. These hallucinatory processes are normal in the infant and help the infant towards the all-important ego function which we call reality testing.

Now there you have the beginnings of an ego, and with that function once under way, other functions are added very rapidly during the first months of life. The first impressions which the infant has are fleeting. They come and go, and they are only distinguished from each other by the connotation of being pleasurable or unpleasurable or painful. But almost immediately the child begins to develop the ability to stir up experience, which means that a past experience of satisfaction is remembered when the same need arises again. The child is hungry again and remembers the moment of satisfaction. This ability to stir up sensations that have happened once—sensations from inside and outside—develops gradually into what is known to all of us as the function of memory.

So now we have an infant able to distinguish between inside and outside and who possesses the function of memory—an all-important function because it guides the child from then onward. But there is one function which only comes into play after a certain time. In the very beginning the child does not distinguish between himself and the environment—they are one—or rather, the child does not know where his own person ends and where the outer world begins. So far as we can determine it from later analytic exploration, we have reason to believe that the child takes the milk bottle or the mother's breast to be part of himself and makes no distinction between his own hand which can be sucked and the breast or bottle which can be sucked too. The only difference is that the thumb, for instance, is always there, whereas the mother or her hand or her breast periodically disappears. So this is the realm where, with the help of the new function of memory, the child gradually learns to determine where his own personality comes to an end. But in the beginning he makes many mistakes in this important business because he takes as the basis for the distinction, not how things really are, but relies again on the sensations of pleasure and pain. The child claims as his own what is pleasurable, and would like to ascribe what is painful to the outer world—a very sensible idea, but it doesn't work in the long run, because the distinction, after all, has nothing to do with the qualities of pain and pleasure. But it takes quite a long time before the child can assimilate disagreeable parts of himself into his picture of himself.

But what is the child's first picture of himself—or, as we can say now, of his beginning ego? When we say 'I' (the equivalent of ego), we know exactly what we mean.[3] We mean our body plus what we know of our personality, which means our body and our conscious mind. One assumes from studies of children at slightly later ages and from studies of adults that, according to all indications, the child first experiences what belongs to his body as himself, as his ego. This is, of course, very obscure territory we are in. The first ego—and this is the way it is put in the literature—is the body ego, built up of the sensations sent by the various parts of the body to the child's awareness. When you observe infants, you will find that they are very fascinated by their own body, that they explore their own body and make gradual acquaintance with it. They are evidently very busy with receiving these sensations from the various parts of the body and building them into some kind of structure for which we have that rather vague name of the 'body ego'.[4] The body ego is, then, the basis of the future conscious personality that collects around it, which has very important contents (of which I will tell you another time). This future conscious personality fills itself with impressions taken from the outside world, which you know about under the title of 'identifications with the outside world'. The body ego is older than the ego which is built up on the basis of identifications. What I am describing to you are happenings in the first year of life—or, rather, in the first few months of life—and I have tried to keep my description as chronological as possible.

---

[3]The use of 'ego' for 'I' (as distinct from the 'other') is one of the meanings given by Freud to *das Ich* and is to be distinguished from the use of the same term for the mental organization (the 'agency') introduced in 1923 in *The Ego and the Id* (1923b, *Standard Edition, 19*) Anna Freud moves from one usage of 'ego' to the other for purposes of exposition, and the context makes her meaning clear.

[4]Now sometimes referred to as the 'body self'.

A further, highly important acquisition of that young ego is now the establishment of a communication between various parts. There is not only a centre of awareness where sensations and perceptions meet, but there is also an attempt to unify these perceptions and sensations, to do something about contradictory impressions. That is, in short, what we call an attempt at integration or synthesis within the ego. We must not place this too early in life; or, rather, we can say it begins early, but early on it only concerns the simplest perceptions and sensations. Then, as the child grows, this synthetic function of the ego proceeds further and further in an attempt to create the unified structure out of the small organ which we later know as our well-functioning adult ego.

It will become quite obvious to you that once this integration of the ego is under way, peace in the child (if there ever is such a thing) is at an end. I described last time how it is one of the important characteristics of id functioning that there is no contradiction between its various strivings. Contradictory in nature as they may be, they live side by side and exist simultaneously. Each urge strives towards satisfaction without regard to the others. When the representatives of these urges meet within the ego, they have to be brought into a sort of harmony with each other, which means that from that moment on, conflict in the human being begins. I do not know whether you have met in literature, in poetry, in history, and every so often in the conversations of people, one particular wish which seems to play a very great part in human beings—namely the wish that one could be a really unified being without inner conflict. One always finds, especially in literature and mythology, these wishful structures of supermen, we might say, who are able to pursue one wish or the other, one aim or the other, without being bothered inside, as if they are moved only by a single purpose. I think that this idea is so widespread because it is so impossible to fulfil it. You might say that the id infant that I represented to you last time is such a superman of single purpose, that he has only one purpose—namely, the fulfilment of his instinctive wishes. But the moment higher development begins, conflicts set in. Conflict and all its consequences are the price paid by human beings for their so-called higher development, which means the division, the splitting up, which occurs within their personality.

Now, what is the good of all these ego functions? How are they used by the infant who has by now grown, let us say, into a child of perhaps a year or a year and a half? There is one more function of high importance we have to take into account—the function of speech. To study the development of speech is in itself a very interesting pursuit. I am no authority on speech; all I have are certain observations on it. If you observe speech development in the infant, you will see that it has roughly two phases. In one phase the infant merely amuses himself—or entertains himself—by trying out the noises his mouth and tongue can make. You will find such an infant lying in his crib and, as the adults say, 'talking' to himself, babbling, crowing, making all sorts of noises, and being pleased with that. That is the first phase. This is very soon then used to establish communication between the infant and the mother. The mother will be the first to understand what the noises mean—or, rather, will recognize them as the expression of a certain mood in the child, a mood pointing to a certain need, and she will answer that need. The mother knows very well that the hungry child, the sleepy child, the wet child, the tired child will produce noises that are of a different kind. These noises change into articulate speech, which definitely serves communication with the environment. It is probably known to all of you from other studies that the understanding of speech comes earlier in the child than the ability to talk—at least for most children. The onset of speech cannot be pinned down to a certain age. There are children who begin to speak at the age of eleven months, and there are other children who reach the age of two and a half before they can speak, the usual age being between one and two years. Psychological studies have shown us that there is a given number of words that children normally use at specific ages, but I know quite a number of people who have not spoken before the age of two and a half (one of them is even here). The parents are often greatly worried about it—but these children usually make up for it later in life by talking a lot. So the acquisition of speech is a very individual process which serves the same purpose—to make the link, the communication with the environment. From the analytic side we know little about what the delay in speech means. It need not mean that this or that particular child is in poor contact with the environment, because the child's understanding of the speech of adults serves the purpose of contact too.

Speech is a highly important function for the child and a very delicate one. If anything happens to upset the child in the two or three months during which speech is acquired, or even three or six months afterwards—if the child at that time is very ill or loses his parents or is sent to hospital or is separated or receives a severe shock of some other kind—speech is usually lost and has to be learned again. I have seen a great number of children who had recently learned to speak and could speak quite well while with their mothers, but who lost their speech when separated from mother and who took months to relearn it. This means that the function of speech is an especially vulnerable one. On the other hand, once speech is acquired, it takes a very severe mental illness indeed for it to be damaged or lost. (I leave out here the slight things that can happen for neurotic reasons, like stammering and other distortions of speech.) But the function of speech is not easily lost in later life, because it is intimately connected with the form of thinking which now becomes the normal form for the growing ego of the child—that is, connected, logical thinking, with all those connections between images which we miss so much in the description of the unconscious. I mean the temporal and causal connections between the thoughts which can only be expressed with the help of speech. From then on, thinking, though it still makes use of images like thinking in the id, proceeds in the ego with words; and that is the enormous difference between former functioning and later functioning, between id functioning and ego functioning.

The ego then uses these abilities to distinguish between inside and outside, to memorize (that is, to store up experience), to distinguish itself from the outside world, to have an integration of its various wishes, to express its thoughts in logical order, and to control its actions. Before the advent of an ego (or before the ego has any strength with reference to the instincts), action proceeds directly under the impact of the drives. Action is meant to bring about wish fulfilment, and action is directed by the drives, without—as I said last time—any other factor being taken into consideration except the wish to acquire pleasure. But now the direction of action is taken over by this new person which has arisen, by the ego, and instead of permitting action to follow directly on the experiences of an instinctive wish, thought is placed between the wish and the action—thought used for the purpose of examining whether the action is appropriate. What would happen in the outside world if that action were to be undertaken? Will it bring danger? Will it harm the individual himself? Will it harm somebody else? And according to its assessment of the state of the environment, the ego now begins to control the inner world—namely, to assess which wishes are safe to fulfil, to what extent, and when. That means that the ego singles out wishes for fulfilment, rejects others, postpones some.

If the little infant that I described to you last time—the infant who acts completely under the direction of his id—had full control of his muscular strength, he would be the most dangerous individual imaginable. He would be a sort of orangutang, striding along and hitting out right and left and taking what he wants. We are only saved from this dangerous individual by the fact that he cannot move, cannot walk, cannot grasp, and has no strength. It is lucky that with the growing bodily strength we get a growing functioning ego which automatically controls that strength. But, of course, we get moments when the id is once more freed from the control of the ego, the moments I mentioned last time when human beings go rabid for some reason, commit crimes, allow their outbursts of temper, become passionate in one direction or another; which means that the direction of action has for the moment slipped out of ego control and has been restored to what it was in the beginning in relation to the id urges—a dangerous situation.[5]

-----

[5]Not all outbursts of the sort described by Anna Freud are eruptions of id impulses. Temper tantrums, for example, while often expressions of the aggressive drive, are often reactions to anxiety, and the aggressive behaviour shown in the tantrum need not be instinctual in origin.

I think it would be a great mistake, on the other hand, if you looked at this gradual building up of the ego as a smooth process, as a process that follows one line without setbacks. Young children learn to control their actions or, as we say, they learn to act rationally, and then their parents expect them always to act rationally; but they don't. Young children of two or three, for instance, are quite unreliable. We do not know whether at a given moment the id will still have control over their actions, or the ego. It is worth enquiring what makes the difference, or how we can predict what will happen. I will give you an example of the simplest kind. In a big city with traffic in the street it is comparatively easy to teach children who are two or three years old the dangers of the road. They know quite well that if they run in front of a motor-car, they will be run over. Why don't we trust them, then—because we don't trust them—to walk on the streets alone? Well, imagine a child of that age—a situation which everybody has seen so many times—walking quite peacefully on the street and even, under guidance, crossing the street in an orderly manner, very proud that he has learned to manage the traffic. But then imagine that same child in the following situation. The mother of the child has left in the morning, perhaps for her professional work; the child is being taken for a walk in the street and suddenly sees the returning mother, at lunchtime perhaps, on the other side of the road. If the child were to be alone, probably nothing would keep him from running over the road to greet his mother, ignoring dangerous traffic. But why? The child knows about the traffic and half an hour earlier could observe the traffic rules. What this means is that when nothing tempting is on the other side of the street, the ego has control of the child's motility. But at the moment when the child saw the desired mother the control slipped away from the ego, and the child's action is controlled by the wish to regain the mother as quickly as possible. This wish now directs action, and the wish has nothing to do with the traffic in the street. All this means that the orderly behaviour, the rational behaviour, of the child depends on a certain relationship which has to do with mental economics. It is a question of relative strength: how strong is the wish, how strong is the ego? At the time when the ego is new and being formed, any wish of a certain strength can overpower it; and this is true for the whole process of childhood. We only regard the process of ego formation as completed when the ego is able to keep control of action and of movement under all conditions, regardless of the strength of the wish, with the exception of those overpowering moments of passion to which everyone is subject at certain times in life. Have you, for instance, ever wondered why young people get their driving licences so late? It's not because they can't manage a motor-car. They can usually manage the driving better than their parents, but the police (who seem to know all about relative ego and id strengths!) do not trust them. They may experience a wish to be somewhere in a hurry, and that overrides the traffic rules. They get their driving licence at a moment when their actions are supposed to be under ego control all the time. That seems to be very late in life.

What, then, does the ego achieve by building up the various functions; what does it bring about in the personality? To repeat: it achieves two extremely important things. The first is to lift the level of the thought processes from the primary process, which I described to you as belonging to the id, to what we now call secondary process: namely, the conscious, logical, rational functioning under ego control—an enormous change. The second all-important function is to interpose conscious thinking each time between the wish and action, which changes the whole appearance of the personality. If you look at it that way, then you will see that the ego has two roles—or we might even say one main role. On the one hand, the ego is of enormous help to the instincts. By knowing the outside world, it can guide the instincts towards fulfilment and particularly towards safe fulfilment. The ego takes regard of reality. It is not any more owned by the pleasure principle. But, on the other hand, by interposing these thought processes and by insisting on safety, reality, and good sense, it holds up and inhibits wish fulfilment. So, while on the one hand the ego is the friend of the id and on the other it seems to be the enemy of the id, in reality it forms the link between the id and the environment.

That is as far as our knowledge takes us today. I suppose you have realized one thing. What I have given you concerning the id and the ego is a framework only—the bare bones of each, two skeletons. I have not told you anything about the content of the id, and I haven't told you anything about the content of the ego. I have told you something about the principles of id and ego functioning and their modes of functioning. And it should now be the work of next week to fill in the empty frames, so that we will begin with the content of the id. I thought it would be helpful to you if you had a structure of the personality first to fit it all in.

Sexuality and development

I feel very different about this audience from the way I felt last week. I know more of what you want, but I have only one real question that was sent to me during the week. It is one that worried me very much indeed, because it showed me that people expected, after presenting the id and the ego, that I would proceed further in an orderly fashion and make you acquainted with the superego. But where should I take the superego from at this point in our proceedings? There is no basis for it. The superego is the product of the forces in the id, and though I have given you the outlines, the principles, the modes of functioning of the id, we have not yet become acquainted with the forces in the id, with the content of the id. So you will have to wait with the superego until we have arrived at the right place.

I hope that the expectation that you might now be able to complete your knowledge of the human personality has not taken away your thoughts from other matters connected with the material—namely, from the question to which we should return after every theoretical excursion. You remember my assignment here is two-sided: on the one hand, it is to make you acquainted with the psychoanalytic theories concerning childhood; on the other hand, it is to point out to you where these theories are of immediate concern to people who deal with the upbringing of children—namely, the parents. And that is an important issue to add to the material that we have had so far. In what way does what we have learned about the id and the structure of the ego relate to the parents? It seems to me that you could use all that knowledge to throw light on one particular point. You have heard it said so often that the most important years for influencing a child are the first five years of life. I don't know whether you have always asked yourselves why, but the answer is contained in the material that I have given you. Think once more of the newborn child as an id with no direct communication with the environment, and then think of the ego as the tool, the instrument fashioned out of the id to bring about that communication. Then you will easily see from my description last time that it takes a number of years before that instrument, the ego, the mediator between inside and outside, the link between the inner world and the outer world, is perfected sufficiently to complete its task. During the time of the immaturity of the ego, the parents step in to fulfil the functions which the immature ego of the child is so far unable to fulfil. This means they have the all-important task of choosing whether a given instinctive wish should be frustrated or should find satisfaction; in the eyes of the child this makes them all-powerful. The task undertaken by the parents is later taken on by the ego itself, and it becomes one of the most important ego functions to control the inner world of instinct, to select what is suitable for satisfaction, to postpone what would endanger the child if satisfaction were to be found immediately, and to modify what cannot find satisfaction in its primitive state. If you then see the task of the parents as being that of a kind of substitute ego for the child, you will also realize how much the attitude of the parents ought to change with the growth in the functioning of the child's own ego. So it is a grave mistake for a parent to continue to try to fulfil these ego functions for a child who already has a mature ego, or a nearly mature ego, and is perfectly able to fulfil them himself. That is when you all become so resentful towards your own parents, when they try to do for your inner world what you like to do for yourself.

So that is just the practical application of the theoretical material that we have dealt with, and it is high time now to give you some concrete idea of the content of the id.[1] What really happens in this underworld? What are those instinctive forces which need the environment for their satisfaction? What is our conception of them?

So far in our lectures I have led you in a more or less systematic way, showing you something about the human personality, without regard to the chronological order in which it was discovered. I now want to go the historical way: namely, to begin where what we call the 'psychoanalytic theory of instincts' has its origin—namely, with the study of the sex instinct. At the same time, I suppose, it is the realm of psychoanalytic knowledge about which you know most, because the knowledge of it is now most widespread. There is a point about it that might be of interest to you. Now that so much knowledge about human sex life has become common property, it is very difficult for the individual to differentiate how much, really, belongs to analytic work, what discoveries psychoanalysis can claim in that realm, and what has always been known.

Well, before it was the subject of psychoanalytic study, knowledge of the sexual functions and the sexual life of the human individual was more or less limited to one aspect only of it. Of course, the importance of the sexual function for adult life, for married life, for procreation, was always known, but it was limited to that. As you may remember (but for you it is old history) sexual life was supposed to begin at adolescence. No knowledge of sexual life was thought necessary to understand

---

[1]What follows is a description, as Anna Freud often put it, 'from the side of the id'. In considering the development of the child's sexuality, emphasis is placed on his move through the various phases of childhood sexuality. It is worth noting that such phases, while they may be appropriate for considering sexual development, are not the best way of looking at ego and superego development, nor at the development of relationships with others—matters dealt with later in these lectures.

children under at least the age of pre-adolescence—twelve was usually the age, and in what was told to parents nothing was included under the term 'sexual life' except genital activity with a partner of the opposite sex leading to reproduction. But what was left out there was a great deal. There were no previous stages leading to this sexual end-result. There was no way of understanding from the theory of sex life, as it existed then, where all the many abnormalities of sex life come from. Even in those times, children before the age of adolescence or pre-adolescence were known to show sexual reactions and to have genital interests. This was ascribed to an abnormal, precocious development, and even though such things were always known to those people who dealt intimately with children—mothers or nurses—they were kept secret; because every mother thought that only her child showed such reactions, and she did not want to expose her child to criticism and blame. So, on the one hand, it was common knowledge, and, on the other hand, common ignorance. But what interested us later was to see that the adult world which did not believe in sexuality before adolescence had still built up very strict sets of prohibitions and precautions against something that was, according to their mind, non-existent.

There are other points: the many inhibitions of sexual functions in adult men and women—what you know as frigidity in women and all the various forms of complete or partial sexual impotence in men—were not understood in those times. They were thought to have an organic basis, to come from the body, not from the mind. And, further, all those irregularities of sex life which are known under the name of perversions, where either the sexual act is not performed on a partner of the opposite sex or not by means of the genital parts themselves—were considered as merely signs of abnormality and depravity, as degeneration of human beings, without any possibility of finding their true causes.

That is more or less the picture of sex knowledge at the point where the psychoanalytic work on it began. If I try to summarize for you what psychoanalysis has added, we still need only a very few headings. It has added, above all, the knowledge that the adult sex life that I have described before is not something 'given' in itself, but the end-product of a long cycle of development beginning at birth and finding its conclusion in adolescence; rather, that these pre-stages of sexuality, as you might call them, are characterized by the fact that other parts of the body, apart from the parts directly serving the sexual function—the genital parts, the sex parts—are involved in it. These other parts of the body are capable of yielding bodily pleasure to the individual of a kind which is comparable, or identical to a certain degree, with that pleasure derived later from the genital parts. These, then, are the very early stages of sexuality about which you have heard and read under the name of 'infantile sexuality' or 'pregenital sexuality'. Curiously enough, the fight about these matters that went on for twenty or thirty years was not always directed against the discovery of these facts—because it is very difficult to deny facts once they are drawn into the light—but they concerned the terminology. The world at large would have been much more ready to accept these psychoanalytic assumptions if only the word 'sexual' had not been extended in its use to cover these pregenital stages, if one had called them something else—'erotic stages' or 'stages of preparation for sexuality'; but the adoption of any of these terms would have obscured the situation in an important manner. They would have denied the fact that these matters play the same role in the life of the child as genital sexuality plays in adult life; and besides, that these are the tributaries which flow together to make up adult sexuality.

I only need to remind you very quickly now of the next bit of knowledge—namely, the building up of the phases of infantile sexuality, centred always around those parts of the body which yield sexual pleasure at the different ages of the child. You may be interested to be reminded of one fact, that none of this was discovered on the child in the first place. It is very curious that an important discovery of this kind was not actually made on the individuals where, after all, it could be seen, but was made during the study of adults who, in the form of their neurotic illnesses, were pointing back to important happenings in childhood. This means the early stages of sexuality were deduced first from material gained on the adult and then confirmed on the child. By now the confirmation has gone so far that everybody can see it, and there are very few people by now who don't believe in it. The direct study of children nowadays, when people undertake it with open eyes, can furnish the same conviction and bring the same material that the indirect study by way of the adult had brought in the beginning.

Now here is the place to put in another question. If all this is so important in childhood, why was it impossible for adult individuals to make this discovery on themselves, with the help of their own memories? Every human being has a good knowledge of his own sexual urges. Why was it impossible for the thoughtful and studious individual to follow that knowledge back to those times before the sexual urges had assumed their adult form? Well, another curious factor comes in here, about which you have surely heard many times—namely, that normally human individuals do not remember their first five years of life, or only very little of it. What happens then are id happenings which are opposed in many ways by the child's growing ego. For reasons of precaution of which we shall hear later, because these early instinctive urges create anxious situations in a child, the memory of them goes by the board or is relegated to the unconscious. And that fact made it necessary to make our studies by the roundabout way of studying abnormal adults, and later by the roundabout way of using a technique of studying normal individuals which leads back to those repressed unconscious parts of the personality—namely, the analytic technique.

But now about the stages of sex development as we find them in the child. They are known to you under three names: the oral, the anal, and the phallic stages. I am quite sure I tell you nothing new with that. This means they are centred during the first year of life around the child's mouth, which is then the source of pleasure; later on around the child's anus, which then becomes the source of pleasure; and approximately between the ages of three and five around the child's genital parts—but around the male child's genital parts and the equivalent in the female. That is why this time is called the 'phallic phase', because it is centred around the penis in the boy and the clitoris in the girl. What does that mean, to say that the pleasure is centred there? And what does it mean that it comes about in such an orderly sequence? Well, certainly it does not mean that at a given date a child ceases to have pleasure from his mouth and becomes interested in other parts of his body; nor is there a sharp transition between the anal and the phallic phase. Probably sensations from all these three parts of the body—sensations of a sexual, erotic nature—are furnished by the body, or demanded by the body throughout the whole of childhood, and the weight shifts from the one to the other in these various stages, with another part of the body coming into the centre of attention. The phases overlap but are still distinguishable.

Well, during the first year of life we know that the child's main concern is the feeding process, and it would be quite wrong to think—though I have met that error in many people—that the only pleasure which the child gains from the feeding process is a sexual one and is therefore what we call a 'mouth pleasure', an oral pleasure. That is certainly not true. The pleasure that the child gains from feeding is the satisfaction of a body need—namely, of hunger. But while the child satisfies his hunger, something happens in his mouth which is extremely pleasurable, which is the first pleasure of that kind we call sexual pleasure; and quite apart from the feeding process, a child who has once discovered that pleasure during the feeding process pursues it further when he has no need for food. We know how children pursue it further. They suck other things beside the milk bottle or the mother's breast. They suck a variety of substitutes, not, as people used to think, because they are hungry, but because they would like to get more of that mouth pleasure which they have experienced during the feeding process. Children, as you know, suck their thumbs or other fingers; some are really greedy and suck two or three fingers at the same time, as much as they can get into their mouth. Some suck their feet, or that part of the foot they can bring to their mouth. Some suck parts of their pillow or an edge of their blanket—there is really no end to the variety of things that can be sucked. We once tried, in a group of about twenty-five sucking infants, to establish similarities in this area, but children seem to have as much variety of taste in their sucking preferences as adults have in the dishes they order in a

restaurant. They have their preferences, and they stick to
them. This means that the child who sucks his thumb would
think that the other fingers are quite uninteresting; whoever
prefers his blanket will not be satisfied with the thumb, and so
on. This sucking seems a very harmless procedure—all the
more harmless since children are very satisfied and quiet when
they do it, so much so that in the last century, for instance, it
was the habit of mothers and nurses to provide children with
something that they can suck—I don't know what it's called
because it has gone so much out of fashion. It's something like
the top of the milk bottle with no milk bottle behind it. [Some-
body in the audience says, 'a pacifier'[2]]. A pacifier—why a
pacifier? Because it pacifies the child's desire for oral pleasure—people just forgot to give the pacifier its full name in those
times. In the last century and in the beginning of this century,
there was an enormous movement, not only against using paci-
fiers but against letting the child have that sucking pleasure
from his own fingers. Children were prevented from sucking by
all imaginable, and for us now unimaginable means—by tying
their hands, by putting bad-smelling or bad-tasting substances
on their fingers, and so on. There were all sorts of ration-
alizations about why one should prevent children from sucking their fingers—that it would deform their upper teeth,
that it would create damage to the skin of the fingers, and so
on. The first battle between child and parent—or child and
nurse in those years—was fought out on the battleground of
sucking. Perhaps now, with our greater knowledge of what is
behind the sucking process, we can guess why this was so,
though probably people were never conscious of it. The child
who is able to pacify his own desires is, to the extent to which
he gains satisfaction in this way, independent of the environment; and it is as if the parents have realized this and claim
strictly that they have the role of deciding when the child
should have satisfaction. The self-satisfaction of the child on
the oral level was considered a menace. If you ask me how long
the pleasure from the sucking process lasts, the answer is not

---

[2]A 'dummy'.

quite easy to find. By rights it should be present in the first and second year, but development is not always as it should be, and you will find children of three, four, and five still sucking their thumbs if it is not forbidden. The other day I even heard of a high-school boy who, after solving a mathematical problem, retires into a corner of the classroom and puts his finger into his mouth. We feel that there is something wrong there. Why didn't the child proceed from this pleasure to the next?

Well, what about the next pleasure? The next pleasure comes, as you also know, in about the second year and lasts perhaps for two or three years. It is centred around the process of defecation and again is not, as many people imagine, merely an interest in the process of defecation or a pleasure connected with the relief that the child experiences when his bowels have moved; children are very much plagued by what goes on in their intestines. Quite parallel to what happens in the mouth, it is the mucous membrane around the anus which yields pleasurable sensations and tempts the child to provide more of these sensations, even when defecation does not take place. But the analogy does not go any further. A question was sent up the other day asking what the symbolic value of excrement, of dirt, is for the child, and this is the moment to answer it. Excrement, the child's own stool, does not have symbolic value for the child. It is valued as such, for its own sake, which is very difficult for the adult to imagine. Here we have an enormous gulf between the feeling of the child about something and the corresponding feeling of the adult. What is to the normal adult a disgusting, dirty matter, and perhaps also a slightly despicable matter, towards which he has a contemptuous attitude, is to the child something very much prized—namely, a part of his own body. The child of two or three who does not know anything of waste-products of the body thinks that this is as good a part of his body as, for instance, his arm or his leg or his hand or his thumb.

The strictness of many parents about habit training may cause the child to lose some of the pleasure he gains from the sensations around the anus. Now children are not given the opportunity to fulfil these anal desires when they are carefully brought up, or very little of these desires only. They shift them very soon to other matters which have some similarity to the product of their body, and the general interest of the child in dirty matter derives from that. Here the question about the symbolic value comes in. For the child, all dirty matter has a symbolic value representing the waste-product of his own body, his excrement. I don't know whether there is anybody among you who only knows clean children. If that should be so, I would like that person to set up an immediate experiment— namely, to collect five children, two and a half years old (if you want to, ten children, but that would make a great noise!) in a room of this size. You can paint the room in very gay colours and you can fill it with most interesting toys, toys appropriate to that age, and then, in the far corner of that room, you put a pail of tar, and then wait a few minutes. . . . And then, if you want to take the time to quantify things, you can see how long it takes the child to leave everything else and get to the tar. It is quite incredible how irresistible the attraction of dirty matter, smeary matter, matter of a certain colour are for children of that age. Probably the attraction is so irresistible because, due to the way in which children are taken care of and brought up, the child is permitted very little of the original anal pleasure.

When, later on, we go into other aspects of the child's development, I will be able to show you that to each of these phases of sex development belong certain aspects of the child's personality; but we will leave that for the moment. I can only tell you (again, it's not news to you) that great change comes about in these dirty little children at approximately the age of three or between three and four, when their interest in anal matters ceases to a large degree and when the sexual sensations centre around the genitals. You all know how the child shows pleasure and interest in that part of the body, by playing with his genitals. Probably it is less clear to you that this interest in the genitals is connected with two very open, manifest attitudes. These are, firstly, a very high curiosity about how other people's bodies are built, especially from the point of view of whether there is a male genital or not, and, secondly, an enormous pleasure which the little boy has in whatever performance he can bring about with his own genital—namely, his first erections. Erections are to be found in little boys at a much earlier age, but at this time they become really important to him, and the admiration for his erect penis, the wish to have it admired by the mother, is the peak of that sex phase. I shan't tell you more about it, because you can find it in the literature—you have probably found it already—and I would like to lead you further.

At the peak of the phallic phase the little boy is very close in his whole makeup to being a little man, closer than he will be for a long time again. Yet just when we would expect this development to go further, and perhaps for adult genital sexuality to grow out of this infantile phallic form, something happens (again something which we will see from another aspect later) to make the instinctive demands of the child quieter. Oral, anal, and phallic pleasures recede into the background, the wishes connected with them become less important, and the child enters into the phase which we call the 'latency phase' because we look at it from the point of view of the instincts which are latent then. Other people call this the 'school age' because at that time the child first passes into the hands of the school authorities. The important thing for us is that at this time the relative strengths of ego and id change place. Whereas in the first period of infantile sex development the instinctive demands have been very strong and the force of the ego directed against them was comparatively weak, the instinctive demands now drop, and that gives the child a chance to develop further, to strengthen itself, to accomplish all sorts of other tasks. The most important of these is learning, in the sense of the development of the intellect.

And now the child, from the age of, let us say, six to twelve or thirteen (it is not the same in all children), begins to resemble the adult in many other ways, no longer of in the forms of his sex activities, but very much so in the fact of nearly being a rational person. Children of this age—latency children—are reliable, more or less, in the way their ego guides their instinctive wishes. And again, just at the time when we think that this individual is really a sensible human being, the child reaches the stage of what we call pre-adolescence, and the whole thing breaks open once more; which means that all the infantile instinctive wishes return. They do not return this time in the form of phases of development, one after the other, but all at once. This means that boys in particular (I am sorry if I sound prejudiced) between then and the age of fourteen or fifteen become once more very greedy, very dirty, and find it quite difficult to keep their bodies reasonably clean. They are very impatient to get satisfaction, very unable to control themselves; and if we examine the form of their behaviour, looking at one item after the other, we can point to all the infantile items which have reappeared from early childhood. So we get this period of revival of infantile sexuality.

And then again, we get a complete change when adolescence sets in, when all these pregenital activities suddenly become unimportant in comparison with real adult genital wishes directed towards a partner of the opposite sex. Such wishes express themselves very soon as real wishes for intercourse with a partner of the opposite sex and are either delayed or find their fulfilment, according to the social class to which the individual belongs, according to the habits of the community. At that time the individual is ready for adult sex life if everything has gone right. But because the way is as complicated as I have shown here, there are many possibilities for hold-ups during the process. At every stage of development there is, as you have seen by now, the problem of demand and fulfilment. How much demand for satisfaction is there in the oral phase, for instance, how much of it becomes fulfilled, how much frustrated? The same is true for the other phases. And hold-ups cannot be prevented by withholding all satisfaction with the idea that the child will then go from one phase to the next because nothing much is being got anyway in the way of pleasure. Children who are denied too much satisfaction in one phase keep a resentment and a hankering after the pleasures of that phase, which means that they become fixed—or, as we say, 'fixated'—to that phase, so that at the time when they should be adults in their sexuality they still pursue their oral or their anal wishes.

'All right,' the world said, a short time after these facts became known, 'let them have all the satisfaction in every stage that they want'. But you know, whenever a child in one of these early phases gets too much satisfaction, he just sits down and refuses to move on, and he acquires a fixation of a different kind. It is perfectly true that the move forward is a biological one, motivated by innate forces, but if the child is very unwilling to leave satisfactions, there is a strong counterforce set up in him, and the end result is the same fixation to the early phases. This puts a very difficult burden on the parents who have to guide the child through this development—namely, the task of determining, in each phase, how much satisfaction and how much frustration is appropriate; that's the quantitative aspect of upbringing through the phases. But further, the parents have also to determine in each phase whether to treat all the pregenital instinctive wishes in the same manner or differently. What you usually find in parents is that either they are very tolerant, and then they are tolerant throughout, or they are very demanding and intolerant, which means that they deny the child satisfaction in all phases. Well, I suppose the qualitative aspect of education in these early years would be for the adult to look closely at each of the instinctive wishes belonging to one of these phases of pregenital development and to determine whether or not there is any place for them later in life. There is a lot of place for the oral wishes later in life, in normal adult sexuality. Every healthy adult uses his mouth, to a certain extent at least, in preparation for the sex act— in kissing, for instance. Apart from the sex act, many mouth pleasures are provided later in life: by smoking, by drinking, by speaking. It is quite different for the anal wishes, which are really excluded from later life, which means that satisfaction given to them very early on might set up attitudes which are quite unusable for the normal adult. On the other hand, the anal instinct, if properly modified at an early stage, brings most important contributions to the adult character. Again this is something we will learn about at a later stage. I would just like you to keep in mind now that it is a great mistake for parents to have this all or nothing, much or little, quantitative attitude; instead, they have to scrutinize the instinctive wishes of the child and correlate them with the way things are in later life.

Where do we normally find the energies of this pregenital sexuality, and what happens to the forms in which it shows itself? Much of it, as you know, finds a place in sex life itself, either as an accompaniment to the genital act or as a preparation for it, and that is perfectly normal. The extent to which this is so varies in different communities. But abnormality begins where one of these forms of pregenital sexuality remains stronger, or becomes stronger again in later life, than the genital wish itself. This now brings us to an understanding of what has always been called the 'perversions': namely, what we see in those adults who find their sexual pleasure not in the normal genital act but in some abnormal act centred around— and you may perhaps be surprised—one of these pregenital forms of sexuality—namely, where the use of the mouth or the region around the anus or some form of exhibition with the penis, with no other use of it, becomes more important than genital intercourse. This means that this study of the pre-stages of sexuality in childhood gives us at the same time an explanation of the abnormalities of sex life which we find in later life. There is a definite affinity between infantile sexuality and the adult perversions. This does not mean that the child is a pervert. Perversions are normal in childhood, just as it is normal in childhood to crawl on all fours, something which is a sign of very great abnormality in adult life.

The inhibitions of sex life, which were so difficult to understand before, equally assume a different aspect when you correlate them with the difficult processes of frustration and denial of pleasure which the child has to go through during his infancy. Any prohibition given to the child during the time of infantile sexuality can remain as an inhibition or develop into an inhibition, and can hold up adult sexuality; this does not mean that freedom given to infantile sexuality guarantees normality in the adult—far from it.

This infantile sexuality—and this is a point that I would like you to retain—is meant to pass. Normal development means experiencing these phases of development in a way which will make it possible to pass through them, to retain only what can be placed in adult life, and to modify the parts which have no place. And that is very much easier said than done.

More on the id

I have received several thoughtful questions since the last lecture, and if you don't begrudge the time, I think I should answer at least five or six of them. This time the questions remained very close to the problems which have been under discussion. In answering them, on the other hand, I become more aware of the shortcomings of my presentations than you probably have while listening to me. In presenting this rather difficult material to you, and in attempting to create an overall picture in your mind, I have, when I move from one step to the next, to make my choice between various possible approaches. In particular we can approach the presentation of the psycho-analytic theory from three sides. We can do what I have been trying to do till now—that is, to give you a structural picture to begin with. Or I could really have chosen a dynamic presentation from the very beginning—namely, I could have confined myself more to an evaluation of the forces which act against each other or with each other. I could even have presented this to you from an economic point of view, quantitatively, so that the personality and behaviour can be regarded as an outcome of the relative strengths of forces which fight it out on the battleground of the ego of the personality. I do vary my approach between these possibilities, but the shortness of time does not give me sufficient opportunity to do so. In presenting to you the picture of sexual development in the human being last time, for instance, I have had to leave the economic point of view for the next lecture. By the economic point of view I mean the idea that what is active in this development of human sexual life is a force, the energy hidden in the sexual instinct, the energy for which we have a particular name in psychoanalysis—libido—and we mean also that whatever happens in the sequence of development, we can view as the fate of the libido. I will try to consider a little of that for you next time.

But now for the questions. I received one important question, asking whether I considered it proper that the study of the abnormalities in human life should lead us to what we consider to be a psychology of the normal. This is a question which has been raised many times, especially in the first years of psychoanalytic history. I do not know whether such an extension is proper; I only know that psychoanalysis is not the only field in science where it happens. The functioning of the normal body is also often studied from the point of view of its pathological distortions. The use of the pathological is extremely important for us, especially in the realm of psychoanalysis, where we do not think it possible to stage experiments—at least not so far as the major events of life are concerned. Psychological experiments will always have to restrict themselves to minor incidents, and we can then perhaps judge the major ones from viewing the minor happenings. It would be too dangerous to interfere with human life for research purposes. On the other hand, in the abnormalities of human nature we are constantly presented with involuntary experiments. Every mental abnormality is at the same time the over-stressing of one variant of behaviour or of one mental causation relative to others; and so we learn enormously about the normal from studying the abnormal. The question, then, of whether we make a proper use of abnormal mental occurrences can be answered by those instances where the observation and experience confirm for the normal person what we have found for the abnormal. And, so far as human sexual life is concerned, this has actually been the case. For instance, the stages of sexual development—or of libidinal development, as they are usually called—have been found in the abnormal, but they have been confirmed over and over again in normal children.

Several other questions put to me were concerned with the details of the various stages of sexual development. For instance, what is the significance of continued thumb-sucking? I have hinted in my lecture that there are certain children who will still persist in sucking their thumbs in their fourth and fifth years, whereas we would relegate that particular form of satisfaction to the oral stage and to what comes immediately after. I think the question of what we consider as the significance of such an occurrence is easy to answer. It is not that we consider the phenomenon highly abnormal, not that such a child is exposed to a particular danger of some kind; but, rather, that we would consider that this child would have given up sucking and would have gone over to one of the later forms of libidinal satisfaction if something had not happened to tie him more strongly than normal to the oral phase. This means that appreciable amounts of sexual energy—oral libido—have remained fixed at that point, and there is a danger for the child that this energy may be missing at later stages of development; which means that his pleasure in later events may be weakened because too much of that particular energy is still busy on an early level.

Another questioner asked whether we have any reason to believe that the child uses the process of defecation as an expression of aggression or contempt. You know that in the adult world, and in the area of jokes and allusions to toilet matters, there is great emphasis on this particular aspect: that defecation, or whatever relates to it, has a contemptuous meaning. It may mean revolt, derision, and especially contempt for another person. Well, I would say that in that respect the little child may in the beginning defecate for somebody, on behalf of somebody—one might say, as an expression of love. Much of the child's training for cleanliness is based on the fact that the mother induces the child to move his bowels at a certain specified time for her sake—we might say, because the mother wants it. She answers to it by expressing her pleasure, as if this were a gift given by the child; and it is actually considered by the child as a gift, as part of his body, perhaps the first gift he can make. When the attitude to the content of the bowels, to all anal matters, is changed to the opposite—which happens very abruptly when great pressure is used, and very gradually when little pressure is used—this gift may change into an expression of the opposite—namely, to an expression of anger, revolt, contempt, derision, and so on.

Another question put to me may have been intended as a question about terminology. Somebody asked why we differentiate between a phallic and a genital phase—after all, the phallus, the penis, is the genital. I tried to explain it when I first used the term by indicating that in the phallic phase the female genital plays no part. For both sexes it is the male genital, or its equivalent in the female, which acts the leading part, and that is why the particular term is used.

Another question leads us far afield and is one which is under discussion in many places. This is whether the latency period, the lessening of the instincts after the fifth year, has a biological basis or is a product of civilization and culture, or perhaps a product of the educational forces converging on a particular child. In a seminar last night I heard the interesting information that in a large number of very different cultures a latency period existed in children. Still this is a question which you will hear discussed very often.

The last communication expresses the hope that I won't simply leave the statement that parents should be careful not to give too much and not too little satisfaction, but that I should, at some point, be a little more explicit about what parents really should do. Well, I will keep that in mind.

Perhaps the last question leads us right back into the time when the psychoanalytic theory of sexuality was first presented to the world and raised a great amount of worry, resentment, and all kinds of disbelief. So far as parents are concerned, there is no doubt that the discovery that something like infantile sexuality exists places a new burden and a new responsibility on them. Their task, from that moment on, in regard to their child has to be looked at with different eyes—they used to think that their task was to protect the child against the sexual influences which might reach it from the outside world. At those times in history when psychological theorists took the view that the nature of the child is essentially good, parents saw themselves as faced only with the task of preserving that goodness in the child and not spoiling it; whereas, as we see now, the task of the parent is a difficult one. It is the guidance of the child past all those stages which are potentially dangerous, because the child might be held back, or might acquire pathogenic nuclei at each stage. But that was probably not the only reason why it took the public a long time to accept these facts of sexual life, with all its ramifications as psychoanalysis sees it, and above all the fact of infantile sexuality. The acceptance of this in the last ten or twenty years has gone very far, and it is now possible nearly everywhere to talk to parents about these matters. In many parts of the world children are treated as beings who have a right to their sexual life, to their sexual instruction, to the help that they need to develop a normal adult sexuality. It is interesting to recall that just the other day a reviewer in a leading English newspaper spoke about the most recent edition of the *Three Contributions to the Theory of Sex*,[1] Freud's book with which all this understanding about childhood sexuality started, and which appeared in the year 1905. The reviewer said that he could really not see why anybody made such a fuss about that book; there was nothing new in it, everybody knew it all anyway. He forgot that it was with that book that our knowledge of all of this started!

I thought that perhaps, after getting this overall picture of human sexuality, you would be prepared to remember a critical accusation which has been made against psychoanalytic theory for very many years (not so much lately)—namely, that psychoanalysis is essentially a form of pan-sexualism, explaining all the facts of life as coming from the action of the sexual instinct. It is curious that this accusation could ever have arisen, because when one goes through the literature of analytic instinct

---

[1] Freud's book was later retitled *Three Essays on the Theory of Sexuality* (1905d, *Standard Edition*, 7).

theory you will realize that psychoanalytic theory has never tried to explain human behaviour—normal or abnormal—as the result of the action of one principle in the mind alone, but, rather, that psychoanalytic theory, instinct theory, has been strictly dualistic from the very beginning, always looking for two principles acting against each other. The first study of neurotic illnesses was certainly not made on the basis that these ill people were over-sexual or that their sexual instinct produced all these abnormalities in them. The view was quite the contrary, that it was the pressure from somewhere else on the sexual instinct, which meant the repression of it, which then led to abnormal symptom formation. What, then, are these principles working against each other in the human mind, as psychoanalysis approached them over the course of years? Well, in the beginning, when human sexual life was studied in this manner, the contrast was seen as being between the action of the sexual instinct on the one hand, and the action of other instincts—hunger is their main representative—on the other, one group of instincts—namely, reproduction—serving the purposes of the species, the other group serving the purpose of preserving the life of the individual. So we had an interaction between two forces represented by hunger and love. That was the very tentative beginning of an analytic instinct theory—one could say, its first stage. After a number of years this proved very unsatisfactory. Theories, as you know, are set up to help to bring order to the facts. Well, this theory did not seem to cover the facts sufficiently, because further studies, I am sorry to say again of abnormal states of mind, led to the finding that the hunger—namely the individual side, what we would now call the 'ego' side of human life—equally played a part in the sexual forces. We will talk more of that next time. It was realized that a sharp contrast between sex and ego could not be made in that form. So the interaction of forces which had various consequences in human behaviour had now to be looked at in terms of an interaction between ego instincts and sexual instincts: two different forms of instinctual life. Aggression, about which we hear so much now, was at that time not counted among the instincts at all but was seen as a reaction of the ego which appeared in defence of wish fulfilment. The view was that in the face of instinct restriction, of frustration, the individual would develop aggression to defend his right to satisfaction.

That was, more or less—I put whole books together here in a few sentences—the next stage. This was followed by a further formation of theory, the one held at present by a majority of psychoanalysts—namely, the theory of the so-called life and death instincts. There is much controversy about that, and to many people the theory seems extremely difficult to assimilate; that is why I thought you might be glad if I said a few words of orientation about it.

The assumption behind that theory is the following. There are two groups of forces active in the human mind. One works towards the unification of life, the construction of life, the building up of ever-greater unities in life. The second force works silently at the same time, trying to undo life, to destroy what has been built up and to lead the individual towards death. You have heard before that the force of the instincts is represented in the human mind by the tensions which are produced, and that the actions leading to wish fulfilment go towards lowering the tensions. If you apply this idea of the pleasure–pain principle to the life and death instinct theory, you would get one group of forces working towards the building up of tension, whereas the other group of forces works towards the lowering of tension completely, so that no life would exist at all. This is a difficult conception, and perhaps you will be very relieved to hear that it is not a conception which really concerns you as psychologists. It is a biological speculation.[2] Most psychologists, when viewing the interplay of forces in the human mind, have formed some theory or other about the instincts which are the cause of it; but by rights instinct theories belong in biology, the actions of instinct are biological ones, and we are only concerned with them in psychology insofar as

---

[2] The idea of a death drive has remained speculative and is not accepted by many—perhaps by most—psychoanalysts. On the other hand, the role of aggression in human behaviour and development, discussed later in this lecture, has been given increasing importance.

the action of the instincts makes a constant claim on the mind and urges the individual to take certain actions. It is with the psychological representation of instinctive life in the mind with which we as psychologists are concerned. For that purpose the speculations about the meaning of these instinctive forces, the understanding of how they are grouped together, and what names they should be given, are of less concern to us.

It seems to me that much confusion has been introduced into psychology and into psychoanalytic psychology by confusing biological speculation with psychological observation. The question we should really be concerned with is: what can we as observers see of this interplay of forces in the mind? How can we define the action of an instinct from the psychological, rather than from the biological side? Well, I think we can see from observation that what the instinct does to the human mind is to exert constant pressure, that it is one of the main functions of the mind to deal with that pressure, and that what we are talking about here are really the methods at the disposal of the individual to deal with the pressures brought to bear on the mind. By the way, this might be an interesting place to remember that it is one of those human ideals which cannot be fulfilled, to possess a mind which is free from the pressures of the instincts, which means free from the pressures of the body. Many practices such as Yoga try to serve the purpose of freeing the mind as far as possible from bodily pressures, from instinctive pressures, because then the mind, according to these ideas, would be free to accomplish the most unheard-of things. Only we forget, when forming an ideal of this kind, that although the mind would then be emptied of energy, the energy would be carried back into the mind from the instincts. I am treating a young patient, a student, a very clever but at the same time a very ill individual, who has as his main pathological concern the wish to be able to function without feeling anything from his body. But, of course, his body takes revenge on him, and just when his mind begins to function properly he is reminded that he has a body by a desire of some kind, by hunger, by his sexual need, by a need from his bladder or his bowels, even by his own need to breathe. This means it is a hopeless task to conceive of a mind not attached to a body. Of course, such a mind, if it could exist, would be free of the demands made on it by the instincts.

What do we know about the instincts then? What can we see from psychological observations? Well, we see that each instinct has a source, and that source is in the body. The various levels of sexual development that I described to you last time were distinguished from each other according to the part of the body which acts as their source: the mouth, the anus, the genital parts, the whole surface of the body; and the skin yields a certain number of sensations of this kind—what we call skin eroticism.

As we have discussed before, what we are talking about is the id. Each instinct not only has a source but an aim. The aim is always the same: to reduce the tension, which means to perform an action of some kind which will fulfil what the instincts are clamouring for—that is, the action of finding satisfaction. And, further, each instinct has an object. Because the aim is the fulfilment of a certain action, the person on whom that action is carried out is the object of the instinct.[3] For the young child, for instance, the mother would be the object, and the finding of nourishment from the mother, the pleasure found at the mother's breast, the pleasure given by the mother's fondling and touching the infant would be the aim. That sounds very systematic and perhaps very superfluous to you, but it will help us later to think of 'instinctual' as actually in that form, that it comes from somewhere, wants something, and needs the help of something or somebody to get what it wants. But then, if we think of what we might call a fight between body and mind, between ego and id, there

---

[3]Here Anna Freud looks at object relationships predominantly from the viewpoint of the instinctual drives. It is necessary to point out that since these lectures were given, increasing attention has been paid to non-drive factors in object relationships, particularly in regard to the child's attachment to objects. The whole area of the interrelation between the child and those close to him is exceedingly complex, and cannot be reduced to libidinal cathexis alone. Nevertheless, Anna Freud highlights a highly important perspective.

is one big factor on the side of the ego, in this difficult task of relieving the pressure that comes from the instinct—namely, that instincts are modifiable in the highest degree. They are not inexorable, although their pressure, if they want something, is inexorable—the pressure is a force that we have to deal with, that we can't do away with. But instincts are willing, for instance—if we now personify them to make talking about them easier—to accept substitute gratifications if they can't have their full gratification. For instance, a child who has some definitely crude sexual wish towards father or mother will accept reduced gratification—will accept affection instead of sexual gratification. We call that an 'inhibition of aim', but it is really a lowering of aim. It is as if somebody wants a very high salary but if he can't get it, well, he'll take less. And instincts are ready to do that, at least under certain conditions.

There are other things to say about the instincts. If the original object—namely, the person on whom an instinct wants to find gratification—is not available, another object may be put in its place. You can think of this as a shifting, as a substitution of one object for the other. Again, the pleasure may be lessened thereby, but it will be accepted as gratification of a 'lower' kind.

And even the aim can be altered. If the child is prevented, let us say, from getting any pleasure from his own excrement, he will be willing to settle for almost the same pleasure from some other less forbidden dirty matter. This is a displacement of aim. There are various forms of displacement about which we will talk later. Further, instincts can combine forces with each other, can fuse with each other, and can part again. They can be directed towards the outer world or towards the individual himself; and they can, under certain conditions, turn into their opposite. It is this quality of the instinct, of being open to modification, which opens the way for the building-up of personality and the forms of character about which we shall hear more in the later lectures. If the instincts did not possess that quality of being open to modification, all these other things could not happen. So I would like you to think of them as being demanding in the highest degree, but on the other hand open to negotiations. And the ability of the ego to deal with the demands of the instincts is dependent on these qualities of the instincts.

Well, I suppose you have had enough of bare bones at the moment. There is an instinct—in our theory spoken of as the representative of the second force in the scheme of the life and death instincts—about which I have not yet given you a picture, and that is aggression. As we see it now in psychoanalytic theory, we look at the sexual instinct as a representative of forces operating on one side, and at aggression as the representative of forces on the other side, both having in our theory more or less equal status as instincts. The study of aggression is certainly not new in psychoanalysis and has not waited for the building-up of these theories. Aggression has always played a great part in the analytic findings, but at first it was considered as a quality attached to the primitive sexual life of the child. The child's primitive sexual life is very aggressive, and, as we see it now, this really comes from the fact that the aggressive instinct develops alongside the sexual instinct. It also comes from the fact that in the various manifestations of life as we meet them the two are inextricably mixed—they are fused. You will normally not find an action of the child which is purely sexual without an admixture of aggression, but you will also not find (except in cases of great abnormality) any action which is purely aggressive without having some admixture from the sexual side. And this can be studied on each level of infantile instinct development, again, in relation to abnormal cases— namely, those cases where either the sexual instinct or the aggressive instinct has been eliminated from the situation by, for instance, severe repression. For some reason the action of one instinct has been inhibited in the child, and we now get the other side of the instinct alone. What about examples? Think, for instance, of the child who eats. On the one hand, he fulfils a body need, on the other he fulfils the urge of the oral drive by incorporating something into his body by way of his mouth and gets mouth-pleasure from it. In the simple process of getting pleasure from food, both instincts are satisfied—the one instinct by the pleasure gained and by the incorporation of the food, the other by possessing and destroying for one's own purposes some substance that comes from outside. But some children are severely inhibited in their eating processes rather early in their lives because they are disturbed by the fact that what they eat is destroyed: by eating, they destroy.

When you look at most human actions, you will find that without an admixture of aggression no sexual action would ever reach its aim. No pleasure can be found with any partner without possessing the partner, perhaps even without subduing the partner to one's wishes to a certain degree, which is an aggressive move. Every one of the sexual pleasures, as they appear during the levels of development (whether it is, for example, the wish to look or to show oneself), always needs a certain amount of active aggression to be carried through to its aim. On the other hand, the aggressive actions of the child, which include all his activities, his actions to mould the outside world to his wishes to a certain degree, to take possession, to find out, to open up: these actions, which are normal when they are fused with the sexual aim at the same time, become purely destructive when for some reason the sexual side is missing. For instance, in recent years we have had the chance to study children who, through no fault of their own, through actions of fate which deprived them of love objects in the outside world, were unable to develop the libidinal side of their nature; which means that their aggression developed without being intermixed with the sexual side. And this aggression in those children appears as pure destruction. They destroy what is around them, they harm themselves, they hurt other people, they get no pleasure from anything except the pleasure of destruction. The force of aggression in these children cannot be diminished in any way unless you induce their other side, their libidinal side, to develop. Then you get the normal fusion between the two instinctive forces, and that leads to normal behaviour in the child.

Where aggression is normal, which means where aggression appears in all the possible mixtures with the libidinal side, it is again like the sexual instinct in that it is open to many transformations. In fact, the most valuable qualities of the human being are introduced into the character (we will hear more about that later, too) by transformation of the aggressive drive, but this occurs only in those instances where the aggressive drive is there in the normal form—namely, fused with the other drive and not in pure culture, as we might say.

You can imagine that there are many instances where two forces in the mind which are so diametrically opposed to each other—sex and aggression—clash with each other. They do not always only fuse peacefully to produce the ordinary forms of human behaviour. They clash, for instance, when sex and aggression in the form of love and hate are directed towards the same person—towards the mother, for instance, or towards the father, or towards the siblings. To the extent that a particular person is loved, the child wants to retain and keep that object. So far as the particular person is hated, the child wants to do away with him or her. According to our idea of the structure of the human mind (and remember what we learned about unification and synthesis within the id and the ego—namely, that there is no synthesis in the id, but there is integration in the ego) this does not lead to conflict in our sense before the child has formed an ego. These opposite urges live peacefully side by side in the undeveloped child. But once an ego is formed and the representatives of these two instincts are brought into consciousness and meet, the child is then under the pressure of severe conflicts, which have to be solved in one way or other; and they are not always solved in a beneficial way.

In the literature you will find other theories which consider that the conflict between the life and death instincts, between love and hate, sex and aggression—whatever you want to call it—exist from the beginning of life, regardless of ego formation.[4] But that is a somewhat different psychological theory, which does not consider ego formation necessary for the experiencing of anxiety. We will learn more about that when we learn more about anxiety.

What I have tried to give you in this lecture and the last is, then, a picture of the content of the id. Whatever psychoanalytic theory we work with, the content of the id is

---

[4]Anna Freud is referring here to the theories of Melanie Klein.

represented by two main forces, by the interaction of these forces with each other and against each other. I wonder whether you have noticed that I have thus far treated the whole process more or less as if it took place only within the child, and I expected a shower of questions in connection with this—questions such as: What about the environment? What is the direction of these forces? What are their objects, what are their aims in the outside? Or, to use the terminology learned here, where is the object world to which the forces existing in the id are directed? Well, our next topic is the building-up in the child of the picture of this object world.

Stages of development

I want to start again with some of the questions which have been sent up to me, because they always show us where we have not sufficiently gone over the ground. Most of the questions are very appropriate in an interesting way.
They show up the places where, if this were not a course serving partly as an introduction and partly as a survey and summary of the subject matter, one would have to stop and give a separate course. They point to all the chapters that branch off from the main line of thought and which we have no time to discuss. But those of you who want to study the subject of psychoanalysis in detail will find that there are many places where you can stop and remain for a long time, by going to the literature and reading the books which treat the subject in detail.

There was one question which was very justified indeed. I made so much, the questioner says, of the stages of development of the sexual instinct, and I rather glossed over stages of development in the aggressive instinct (if, indeed, I talked about them at all). What about them? Are they comparable in intensity, in distinctness, in sequence, to those of sexuality? Well, one answer to that might be the following: the intensive study of the development of aggression began long after the study of the development of the sexual instinct—perhaps thirty years after it—and our knowledge has not yet reached the same level. This means we know very much less about the stages of development of aggression, or, rather, we tend to view them very much as intimately connected with the sexual levels of development. On each level of infantile sexual development the aggressive instinct appears in a different form, always closely linked with the sexual urges. We do not know whether it takes its cue from them, whether the level of sexuality reached colours the form taken by the aggressive urge or whether it is the other way round, with definite stages of aggression giving a particular character to the levels of sex development. It probably goes both ways, because (as I tried to show you last time) the two are very intimately linked, and in whatever the child does—whether it is an expression in the oral stage or in the anal phase or the phallic phase—we find aggression and sex linked together. We see this, for instance, in the sadism of the child, which is partly an expression of the aggressive instinct— especially in the anal phase—but which is above all an outlet for aggression. So this is a question which awaits detailed study.

Then there was one complaint. When talking about the object and the aim of an instinct, the questioner says, the two got a bit mixed up. What is really the difference between an object and an aim, and are they not both the same? Well, that is merely a matter of terminology, so I shall just repeat what I perhaps did not say precisely enough. We call the aim of an instinct the particular activity which serves the instinct's satisfaction, and we call the object of an instinct the particular person—in the outside world mostly, but not always, as we shall hear later—on whom this particular activity is performed. So that is object and aim, or, rather, those are the terms, and we use them for convenience. Of course, you could decide to say that one particular activity is the object and the other is the person, but what I have described is the way we use the terms in psychoanalysis.

Another questioner asked why conflict in the human personality should wait for the establishment of an ego? Is not conflict always there before—this means conflict between the instincts—before the ego has been set up? Is it not only that the conflict does not become noticeable before that time? Well, this is, of course, perfectly true. If you use the word 'conflict' for the coexistence of urges which in our mind are not compatible with each other, then conflict is there from the beginning. But if you use the term for a very specific state of mind felt by the person—that is, 'being in two minds' about something—then conflict has to wait for the ego where these incompatible urges meet. This means you have to wait for the time when there is integration within the personality, when there are organized processes.

A further question has to do with children who are separated from their families at very early ages, like the children I have described in some of my publications. Are the phases of sexual development the same in these children, or are these phases of development influenced by the actual experiences in the environment of the child? Well, that is one of the points where one has to stop and either write or read a book about it. Because both statements are true. On the one hand, we look at these phases of development, after having studied them in a great number of children, as something which is to a certain degree independent of outside influence, as something for which the child is predestined in some manner, which to a certain degree is innate in the child, which is a process of maturation. But on the other hand, it is perfectly true that the progression of these stages, the length of time which they persist, the role which they play later in life, has something to do with environmental influences, which means that there is a meeting at each stage between inner preparation in the child and outside influence.

And then there is a question touching on the problems of adolescence. Of course, one should stop here again and study more about adolescence, because what I have tried to say in one sentence only—that in adolescence, or at least in the preparation for it, in pre-adolescence, the problems of early childhood return—is no more than a chapter heading covering very interesting facts. Our questioner wants to know whether in adolescence, when these infantile sexual and aggressive problems return, the attitude of the ego towards them is reduced once more to that role it had taken in early childhood, when the outside world has to step in to large degree and take over the control which the ego should exercise itself. And that is a definite misunderstanding of the facts. That is my fault, because I did not make it clear that one of the great sources of suffering in adolescence is the fact that this crude infantile instinctive life returns at a time when there is an ego, and, as we will later hear, a superego. And these two—ego and superego—retain their characteristics in the adolescent phase, so that whereas the ego of the young child was tolerant towards these instinctive urges, the ego of the adolescent is not at all tolerant. This means that the adolescent suffers acutely from the return of the infantile instinctive world, whereas the small child is not the one who suffers; rather, it is the parents who suffer as a result. (Of course, the parents of the adolescent suffer too—we should say that both suffer.) The adolescent is firstly in conflict with himself, and secondarily in conflict with the environment.

What I would like to do today is to go once more through the stages of development which I have described to you recently, but from a different angle—namely, with the question in mind about what the forces we have to deal with in the child really are. That subject leads us to ask again what the task is that is involved here for the parents. Is it an easy task or a difficult one? Is the sexual life of the child something that can be moulded, guided, influenced by the parents, that can be easily suppressed by outside influences? Again, the answer has to be yes and no. It can be influenced, it can be harmed, it can be modified, but it cannot be eliminated from the life of the child. Nothing the parents can do will do away with it. I sometimes find it useful, when I want to explain to a parent what an enormous force the instinct is in the child there, to draw their attention to one small item in which this instinctive life of the child is expressed. That might be, for instance, thumb-sucking. It might be other activities which the child performs on its own body, for instance, masturbation in the phallic phase. It might at some other time be a particular hobby of the child, some interest in which the child's sexual curiosity expresses itself. Each of these single activities has behind it the full force of the sexual instinct of the child. If you take a thumb-sucker or perhaps a nail-biter, nothing in the world will make him stop. The parents can use violence, they can use love, they can plead and beg, and they can use threats, but the child cannot stop it. Each of these activities, so far as it is carried by that instinctive force, is indomitable in some way in its strength. Well, what is this strength that we see here, what is this force? We can regard it as the energy underlying the sexual urges, and as you know we have a special name in psychoanalysis for it—we call it the 'libido' or the 'libidinal energy' of the child, which merely means the energy of the child's sexual activities. We speak in the same manner of the energy underlying the aggressive urges of the child without using a special name; we merely speak of 'aggressive energy'. It is the flow of this energy which we have to try to observe in the child if we want to have any chance to guide and influence it. In doing so the parents have to guard against two mistakes: against underrating the aggressive instinct—well, the child will soon teach the parent better; but we also have to guard against overrating it, by saying, 'well, if that wish in the child is so strong, nothing can be done about it, the child has to have its way. I do not want to harm my child by opposing either his sexual or his aggressive wishes'. This is, as you know, a very common attitude of parents in our times. It is the so-called permissive attitude. But parents who take this line thereby renounce all hope, not only of opposing the instinctive urges of the child but of helping the child to modify them. The child has to modify the instincts in the course of time because most of them find no place in adult sexual life or, so far as aggression is concerned, in the adult community. Detailed study of the fate of this instinctual energy, especially the fate of the libido, is therefore our only safe guide in this difficult matter. Again, I am presenting to you knowledge which has not been found directly from children. Much (but not all) of it has been confirmed from direct observation, and much has been found from adults, normal and abnormal. This is because the fate of the instinctual energy does not only determine character formation, which means the development of the child in the early years, it also determines the normality, the abnormality, the happiness, and the unhappiness—of the adult human being.

How do we imagine, then, that the whole thing looks in the beginning? Perhaps I had better first say a word about the quantities with which we have to deal. We talk a great deal of quantities in psychoanalysis—quantity of libido, quantity of aggressive energy, and so on. We speak of 'sending' this quantity here or there, of 'charging' an object with it, for which a Greek word is used in analytic terminology, the word 'cathexis', which merely means, if you compare it with electricity, that a certain amount of that energy is sent out to a certain person or material object. I have never liked that term, but the translators have found no better one.[1] We talk, then, of quantities, but we are not able in our particular science to measure these quantities. All we can do is to compare them with each other. We compare, for instance, the quantity of libido with the strength of the aggressive urges; or we compare libidinal strength with the force the ego has at its disposal. But we talk of it, not mathematically, but more in an allegorical way, measuring two forces against each other in their battle with each other. And these inner conflicts in the personality are very often decided, not by the quality of the urges which are fighting with each other, but by their respective quantities.

It is time now to make that more concrete. If we imagine that a child is born with an innate sexual drive and is moved from the beginning by this drive, we see—again from experience gained in later years—that there are two possibilities for the child to use this libidinal energy: he can use it on his own person or on persons in the outside world. In ordinary terms we would say the child can love himself or he can love a person in the outside world, and the person or the self charged, cathected in this manner with libidinal energy is the child's love object. So that we have, from the beginning, two possibilities: sending

---

[1] EDITOR'S NOTE: The original German word is *Besetzung*, and 'cathexis' is, indeed, an unhappy translation. Perhaps 'investment' would have been better.

libido out into the environment or keeping libido inside for the child's own body and, as the ego and superego grow and increase, directed towards the ego and superego. So from the beginning we get two possibilities: self love and love for others. For self love I want to introduce another term which may be quite familiar to you—namely, 'narcissism'. We can differentiate then between narcissistic libido and object libido. We can say that the life of the child is really decided by how his narcissism and his love for the environment stand towards each other.

How does all this look in our actual experience of infants? You remember that I said that for the infant, contact with the environment begins on the basis of his bodily needs. He is hungry and wants to be fed, and if he is fed he experiences satisfaction. These first satisfactions that he experiences show the way, provide the direction in which he is going to send his libido. That sounds complicated, but it is terribly simple. If we put it in words, we would say, the child feels, 'this is nice, I like it'. The experience of satisfaction is followed immediately by a sending-out of libido towards the environment, towards the particular object or person who has provided that satisfaction. Satisfaction, then, shows the way to libido attachment. But the child does not always find satisfaction in the outside world. The same bottle which gives milk at one time may be empty at another time, perhaps immediately afterwards, before the child's hunger is really satisfied. So it is not a nice bottle any more, it is either an indifferent or an unpleasant bottle. Or the same mother who has fondled the child leaves the room or turns away, which means that for the child she is no good any more, so far as satisfaction is concerned. It seems highly important that in the moments of dissatisfaction, when the object in the environment is no good, the child withdraws the libido which he had sent out and uses it once more on his own person, only to send it out again towards the object world when satisfaction is offered and the environment is pleasant. This means that there is a continual change of narcissistic libido— self love, into object libido—love for others, and change from object love back again to self love, and so. This happens constantly in the earliest part of the child's first year (at least, that is how we picture it on the basis of later experience). I would like to give you one little example which you can find in children a year older, something which impressed me very much when I first saw it. If you have ever had to feed children of approximately sixteen or eighteen months who can already eat on their own, who don't have to be spoon-fed any more, who use a cup, a plate, a saucer, and other implements, you will have found a curious and interesting phenomenon. They hold their cup, with milk or cocoa or whatever they drink from it, and handle it quite carefully and skilfully. But when it is empty, and if you are not very quick, they throw it away (it's very good to have plastic cups and saucers!). You surely have noticed that. Now, what is the child doing there that we don't do? The child, at that ripe age of eighteen months, evidently can give up his regard for the cup when the cup is empty. Then it is thrown away, it is no good; and this gives us a very good picture of what the child does with his love objects, at least up to that age. He cannot retain his relationship to them when they are emptied of the satisfaction they could offer. He throws them away—but that is something one can only do with a real cup. Where love objects are concerned, the child withdraws his libido cathexis from them, which is as good as throwing them away. And we consider this phase, in which the child treats his objects—above all the mother, or what she has to offer—in that way, as a sort of preparatory phase for what we call object relationship. It is a phase in which the object for the child consists only of something which is able to fulfil a need. It is the phase of 'the need-satisfying object', as some people call it. This need may be a material need—for instance, for the appeasing of hunger. It may be (and this comes very soon in the child's life) a need for affection, for being comforted, fondled in all sorts of ways. Whatever the need is does not change the essential basis of the relationship—namely, that the relationship is inconstant and ceases with the satisfaction, and is begun again with the renewal of the need.

Then comes the next phase in the child's life, in which he behaves in relation to his cup and saucer as we do. We keep them for the next meal and handle them carefully or even cherish them, whether they serve momentary satisfaction or not. Now the child begins to do the same with his mother, which means his attachment to the mother—the libidinal cathexis of her—remains constant regardless of the need. This phase, then, would be the phase of object constancy and is already very much nearer to what we regard in adult life as a proper love relationship or emotional relationship to another human being. But even in this phase of object constancy it takes a long time before the child sees more than a provider in that person in the outside world. It takes a long time until the child begins to see that this is a person too, a person with his own rights, his own needs, his own demands, and with whom the child becomes able to 'interchange' affection, love, emotion—namely, not only cathect the object with libido, but on the basis of that cathexis consider the object with the same regard that the child has for his own self. Once this has occurred, then we have what we would call a real object relationship in that particular child.

It may become clearer to you that studying these phases is more than of purely theoretical interest when you realize that these various stages and levels of relationship to our fellow beings are reflected very closely in adult behaviour. We all know that the desirable adult behaviour towards our fellows should be on the basis of this last stage of object relationship—namely, where there is consideration and regard for the object with an interchange of feelings. But there are many instances, and many forms of abnormality, in which adults regress to earlier levels of object relationship and see in their friends—in their sexual partners, for instance—nothing but the provider, and only love them for the satisfaction they can get from them. And we know that types of disturbed adult regress to that first phase of inconstancy in love relationships, where objects are thrown away, figuratively speaking, or emptied of cathexis when the satisfaction from them is over and a new object is sought for renewed satisfaction. So these phases of development in the child's love for the mother reflect at one and the same time the whole range of possibilities of disturbance in adult love relationships.

I know there will certainly be someone who will send in a question asking: what about aggression at the same time? And here again I have to say that our studies of the paths taken by the aggressive instinct are not as detailed as those of libidinal cathexis. But we do have an idea from what we have observed up to now that aggression follows the choice of object made by the libidinal urges, made by the sexual side, very closely. This means that the love objects of the child are also the hated objects, those who have to bear the brunt of the child's aggression. There is a further item to be considered on the aggressive side. Whenever the child is refused libidinal satisfaction, he responds with aggression. We do not know whether this aggression merely serves the purpose of defending his libidinal interests. It would be quite understandable if it were so, because it is also what we know from adult behaviour. It is also true that where the libido does not find satisfaction, the aggression pushes itself all the more into the place of the other instinct. We do not know whether a child who has none of his wishes frustrated would not be aggressive, because it is impossible to exclude the experience of frustration in a child's life. It is probably something we would like to try to discover through experiment, but since there is no such state as constant libidinal satisfaction, we cannot get our proof. As a result you will find many people in the psychological world who refuse to believe that aggression is really as basic, as primordial, as the sexual instinct in the child and assert that aggression is merely produced by experiences of dissatisfaction. As I told you last time, I hold the other view—namely, that sex and aggression are both basic instincts. But I readily concede—and you can all observe it whenever you deal with young children—that over and above the aggression which may be present in the child from the beginning, those amounts produced by frustration of libidinal wishes play a very great part. There you more or less have the position.

But, then, who are the people in the environment on whom all this play of sex and aggression of the child is actually 'acted out', as we say? Well, I have named the mother very often, but that is not quite correct, because in the beginning the child is not concerned with the mother. The very young infant does not have the possibility of conceiving of the mother as a person. What he is concerned with are those parts of the mother which serve to give immediate satisfaction. Such parts may be the mother's breast, the mother's hand, perhaps the mother's face: the breast giving nourishment, the hand giving pleasure to the surface of the body, and the face and the mother's smile serving the purpose of reassurance, of comforting, of quietening the child. And in the phase of lack of object constancy, of breaking off relations ever so often—what we call the phase of 'the need-satisfying object'—it is such parts of the person which play a significant role for the child. And as the child matures, as his ego functions become more complete and his recognition of the outside world better, he takes in more of the mother, until the whole person of the mother becomes the object of his interest, of his sexual interest, of his aggressive interest. He then really has become attached to the person of the mother. This is not an easy time for the mother, when she is claimed for the first time as a whole person by the child. Because the child claims her as if there were no one else in the world except the two of them. Now no mothers—or very few—live alone with their young infants. The whole set-up of mother and infant occurs within a family, which means that there are other people who play their part and who claim the mother's attention, who claim her love and interest as much as the infant does. Which is the first insoluble conflict for the young infant, and the first misunderstanding between the environment and the child. I say this because for the child it is impossible to conceive why this mother should not belong to him exclusively, to love and to hate, to play with, to have, to satisfy himself on; whereas to the mother it must be just as inconceivable that she should belong to that one child only. And naturally to the father and the other children it does not make sense.

There is one way, though, in which every normal mother meets the demands of the infant, at least in the first few months of life. When people discuss the position of a new child born into the family and the jealousy which older siblings must feel on that account, there is always talk of reassuring the older child—for instance, the child of two or three—that in spite of the new baby's arrival, his mother loves him just as much as she has loved him before. And we wonder why young children find it so difficult to believe that, and why they always act for a time, whenever the next sibling is born, as if they had lost their mother's love more or less completely. I think they act that way because there is a grain of truth in it. For the young mother, every newborn child is something very specially hers, very much a part of her body still—which, after all, it has been for a very long period—very much belonging within the framework of her own self-love, part of her self, and therefore loved in a very peculiar way. Which means that more or less every normal mother is ready to belong, for a short while at least, for a few months, to the newborn baby exclusively, even if she makes every conscious effort not to withdraw any love from the older child. This is a difficult situation, and every mother of more than one child knows it very well.

The question is very often raised of what the role of the father is in that first year of life. Under less modern conditions fathers used to have very little to do with their newborn babies. They used to look at them from a distance, they would complain a good deal about the disturbance which the baby created in the house, and they used to resent the fact that the child took so much of the mother's attention away from them. Under modern conditions this has changed a good deal, and many fathers take part in the bodily care of the baby; this means, as we would say, that these fathers offer themselves to the infant in the role of a need-satisfying object, the role usually only taken by the mother in relation to the baby. But where the father does not actually share in the baby's care, the relationship to him begins on quite a different level. It begins a good while after the mother relationship has been firmly established, and the relationship with the father usually begins in two ways at once. One of these is a direct way: object libido is sent out to the father, no longer because he is need-satisfying in the bodily sense but because he is liked and admired for certain of his qualities, for certain things which he can do which the mother cannot do. So he becomes a direct object of affection to the child, an object of admiration, sometimes of aggression. But at the same time, invariably in the normal family, he becomes a rival. The baby and the father have rival claims on the mother; and that begins quite early. I only talk of those fathers (I have to be very careful about fathers because they are very touchy nowadays) who do not care in a bodily way for their babies, and whom the baby probably won't notice much before the second year. If the father feeds the baby, dries the baby, and washes the baby, that will be different.

So, on the basis of constant object relationships, we now have, in the second year of the child, three elements. One is the positive and a negative attitude to the mother—loving and hating her according to her behaviour towards the child. Then there is the same kind of attitude towards the father; and the third is the distinct rivalry with the father. The libidinal situation naturally becomes complicated for the growing baby where there are older siblings in the family, and we can now study these various shades of relationship; because the same kind of rivalry that exists with the father naturally exists with the siblings. But this is less full of conflict for the child because the siblings are less loved. They are in the first place rivals, and only secondarily companions.

It is interesting to see that situations of this kind are open to a great deal of variation according to environmental circumstances. It has been possible recently to observe the libidinal relationships of children towards other children of the same or nearly the same age, which means towards contemporaries in the position of siblings, in the absence of parents. To our surprise it has been fully confirmed—at least in those instances which were open to observation—that under these conditions children do not seem to develop the jealousy of their contemporaries which seems so normal and natural to us under usual family conditions. This means that the child is not jealous, does not hate his brother or sister because they both want the same thing and can't have it or because the other children take something away from the child—they take his toys or destroy his games, but do so quite explicitly, because these other children are rivals for the love of father and mother. Where this basic rivalry in the family is absent, children can love each other—which is a very curious fact, because siblings certainly do not love each other. You will say that is not true, but the truth is that they learn to love each other in later years. And, again, they learn to love each other on the basis of something very curious; they learn to love each other because they belong to the same parents. And when each child has his full libidinal object relationship to the parent and has reached the stage where sacrifices can be made, the child begins to like his brothers and sisters because they belong to the mother, just as the child learns to like the mother's dresses, the mother's coat, and the mother's implements in the house, and to spare them rather than destroying them. So the love of siblings towards each other goes by way of the love of the parents, just as the jealousy of the others goes by way of the love of the parents. The relationships look completely different where children, in the absence of adult love objects, send out their libidinal cathexis directly to their contemporaries—a most abnormal state, but very useful to us for the purposes of study.

These matters are complicated, and I did not want to summarize them too much. I want next time to take you at leisure through the forms which the love and hate relationships of the child can take, following through the libidinal and aggressive stages of development, and then to take them to their peak in the family situation—namely, to the so-called Oedipus complex.

Love, identification, and superego

The phases of development of the child and the various stages in his relationship to people in the outside world are what have been worked over most in psychoanalytic theory and practice. There is therefore a vast amount of data in this field, and it is a field in which those people who deal with the analytic theories of child development stay for more or less all their working lives. To speak for only one or two hours on these matters means a great effort in summarizing, and it is only natural that very important parts of the whole matter have to be dealt with as if they were only of minor, secondary importance; and much has to go by the board. I can only try to do my best about it, but no best can be good enough.

If, for instance, you consider the period in the child's life which I tried to deal with last time, you will realize that included in it is an enormous advance from a close intimate relationship between one small human individual and one other person (the mother), a relationship confined to an interchange of the most primitive kind. And then, up to the third or fourth or fifth year, there is the widening of the relationships to a number of people, with enormous variations in that whole process which we speak of under the name of 'object relationship'. The advances which a child makes during that time, from being a small, primitive, instinctive, animal-like being to the nearly complete apparently adult person—because the child of five in many respects gives a picture of an adult person—are enormous. And when one has the opportunity to watch this change closely, either in one's own children or in children who are under one's observation, one is always surprised at where the advances come from. I have been in the position where I have seen children day after day, where I was controlling their environment and had full knowledge of their environmental influences, and again and again I have seen reactions arise in these children which were quite surprising to me. We are confronted over and over again with the question: where does that change really come from? This means that what we see in the child is not merely a result of environmental influence which evokes a response from the child. These environmental influences, acting on the basic inborn personality, are worked over within the child and appear on the surface as something completely new, a process which is fascinating to follow but not so easy to describe in concise terms.

At the end of the last lecture we left the child at approximately at the age of three or four with a number of distinct relationships formed in his mind. There was no longer the exclusive relationship to the mother, but the object relationships (which means the attachments to the outside world) had been extended to include a second parent-figure, the father, and also included the siblings, the brothers and sisters; and each of these relationships had a very distinct separate form. You remember that I tried to characterize in a few words how the ambivalence towards the mother is of a different nature from the ambivalence towards the father ('ambivalence' is the term we use when the child has positive and negative relationships towards the same person). The negative feelings towards the mother are based mostly on those instances where the mother fails to give the child satisfaction, whereas in the relationship to the father there is the added role of the father as a rival. In the relationship to the brothers and sisters the rivalry takes first place, and the positive relations to the companions, to the playmates, comes afterwards.

You may remember, if you think back to the lecture in which I tried to explain something of what we call the 'theory of libido distribution', that we found two ways in which the child uses the libido, the sexual energy at his disposal. On the one hand, the child attaches it to his own body and his own person for the purposes of self-love, or narcissism; and on the other hand, the child uses this same energy for his attachments to the outside world—namely, for the purposes of object love. This is an important concept, which we will need in the lectures to come. There is a constant exchange in the normal child between one type of use of the libido and the other. I mean that whenever an object is unsatisfactory, or whenever the love relationship to an object is interrupted for some reason, the child uses that part of the libido previously attached to the object for attachment to his own person. So there is a continual exchange between self-love and love of others.

We now have to add to these types of libidinal use and libidinal behaviour in the child two sorts of relationship to the objects in the outside world. Envisage, if you will, in your own mind the mother, the father, and the siblings as the prototypes of three sorts of object relations with the environment. Then the matter is complicated further by the fact that the child does not merely have what we call an 'object attachment' to these three 'sets' of people, but has as well a second type of relationship of which you have certainly heard a great deal—namely, an 'identification' with them. I have reminded you once more of the idea that object libido can be changed back to narcissistic libido, because we need to understand this process in order to understand the nature of an identification. It is really a very curious thing that happens here. Let us imagine the child now in his relationship to the mother, in one of those situations I described before in which the mother is unable to satisfy the child either with food or love or with her presence. I have said that is the moment when the child withdraws love from the mother and uses it on himself, but now we want to learn more about this process. The child is able to withdraw from the

mother in a very curious way only—namely, by erecting somewhere inside himself, within his ego, a picture of that part of
the mother with which he had dealings just before. Something
of the mother figure, of the mother image, is carried inside and
built up inside the child, probably on the basis of a wishful picture. Do you remember those wishful images which the
child creates at the beginning of life when any instinctive urge
arises in him? The urge brings with it the picture of the fulfilment and of the object on which fulfilment should take place. It
is probably in this way that the child who is dissatisfied with
the mother now attaches his libido to the image of the mother
inside, and this image of the mother inside is now 'cathected',
as we say—charged no more with object libido but with narcissistic libido. It has become part of the child, and the mother is
now a picture inside; the child is trying to get satisfaction from
the picture, instead of from a real mother outside. We might
say that part of the child has changed so as to represent the
mother for purposes of satisfaction.

So this process of changing object libido into narcissistic
libido is accompanied by a continual development of identifications. That is actually the way in which the child's ego enlarges,
grows, fills itself with content. If you remember the lecture
about the ego, you will also remember that at that time I spoke
of the ego merely as a group of functions, perfected to fulfil
certain tasks relating to the outside and the inside worlds.
But now we are talking of a different aspect of the ego
altogether—namely, of the ego as the kernel of the personality
containing what we claim as ourselves. This very personal person that we carry inside is made up out of bits and pieces of the
people whom we loved as little children. This is a curious process, well worth thinking about, and, indeed, a great deal of
work has been done to find out more about it, to catch the child
in the action of identifying, and to determine, after identification has taken place, in what way the identification has come
about.

We have therefore the child in the centre of a small group
of people around him, the nearest members of his family,
attached to them by object love on the one hand, and on the
other hand continually identifying with them. In this way he

builds up a person who is, we might say, similar to them, but the bits and pieces taken from the outside world get so inter-mixed that it is very difficult, except through a personal analysis, to decide where each single piece has come from. You all know the situation when an interested aunt looks at a child and says, 'Well, the eyes are the mother's, and the nose, that's the father's, and, you know, the mouth is the grandfather's.' We smile about these attempts to find the features of the parents and grandparents and uncles and aunts in the child's face, though there is often, of course, a great deal of truth in what is seen. There is certainly a great deal of truth in it on the mental side. All the pieces which now make up the child's ego have belonged to others, and it is a great mixture of attitudes, of qualities, of prohibitions, of commands, of ideas, of wishes, which the child collects; and the child has the task of making one harmonious whole out of it. Perhaps if you look at the process of identification in this manner it will become also clearer to you why it is so difficult for children whose parents are in a marriage full of conflict to build up a harmonious ego. If the bits and pieces which the child takes over from the out-side world are conflicting in the outside world, they will be very difficult to harmonize inside. The same is true in cases where the child is dealt with by more than one person in the earliest months of life. The younger and cruder and simpler the organ-ism is, the more beneficial it is for the child not to have too many objects of identification. It is better to build up these first inner images, these first parts of his personality, on the basis of a single or a very few relationships only: one relationship first, two relationships afterwards.

An appropriate question to ask now would be whether the siblings serve the same purpose. Do we really, besides having those pieces of our father and mother inside us, also have all these little pieces of our brothers and sisters? Well, yes and no. Where there is a big difference in ages, bigger brothers and sisters can play a role for the child of, we might say, reduced parents; they are then treated also by identification, as with the parents. But where siblings are more or less contemporaries, these identifications take place very much less or are much less important.

There are two important questions now. What determines the importance of an identification? By 'importance' I mean the role which this identification is destined to play in the child's later life, because these identifications are very difficult or impossible to get rid of. This is one of the analyst's tasks later in life. The second question is: what are favourable and unfavourable conditions for identification? Which is again what Professor Sears' work is about.[1] It is not so difficult to discover what determines the power of an identification. It is in direct proportion to the power and strength of the emotional relationship which has preceded the identification. A passionate relationship of the child to father or mother or both will bring strong identifications. The power of the identification will in a sense be the heir to the strength of the relationship. It is one of the adverse factors affecting the fate of those children who, through the absence of parents or through the poor quality of the parents, have not had the opportunity to form strong object relationships to them, that the identifications of these children are weak and powerless. Their egos remain somehow defective, less satisfactory. However, it would be a mistake to think that the power of the object relationship is in direct proportion to the permissiveness of the parents. It is not true that the child loves the permissive parent more than the restrictive parent. To our surprise, we very often find the opposite. It would lead us too far away here to discuss why. But when you study identifications, you will find that they are usually made in states when the child has been dissatisfied with the parent. This would mean that a greatly loved parent, the relationship to whom is interrupted by frustrations—all the inevitable frustrations which the parents have to impose—would probably be the object of the strongest identification. On the other hand, a parent who tries to be permissive all the time will probably maintain the child's attachment, his object relationship, to a degree which leads much less to a frequent or continual process of identification. After all, why should one not leave the object in

---

[1]The reference here is to Robert Sears, who was one of the first to test psychoanalytic hypotheses experimentally.

the outside world if the object is so highly satisfactory, is such a continual provider of satisfaction? It is the taking of the object inside which represents an attempt to continue the role of provider from inside.

I think this is the moment to remind you that when I gave a picture of the structure of the human personality, I stopped after describing two parts of it—namely, id and ego—and I said that I had nothing yet to say to you about the birth of the superego. Well, this is the moment when you can see where the superego has come from. What we call 'superego' is nothing more, and nothing more mysterious, than the result of these first identifications of the child. Because the first loves of the child are the most powerful ones, the first identifications— those of the first years—are the most powerful. They retain a separate position within the ego from then onwards, and it is this separate position, this added importance and power, this glorification of the first identifications within the personality, which we designate as the superego. There is no superego except on the basis of identification with the parents, and there is no identification with the parents—at least no identification leading to a superego—except on the basis of love for the parents, of object attachment to the parents. This means that the superego is born of the object attachments to the parents, and that explains certain qualities of the superego. If we only hear the term 'superego', we could easily be led to think that this formation within the ego is in all respects superior to the ego where all functions are concerned: for instance, that it is more reasonable than the ego. But that is certainly not the case, and it would be a great mistake to think so. The reasonable part of the personality is the ego, and it remains that way. The ego has been built up as a result of the struggle with outside reality, for the purpose of knowing and partly dealing with it, but the superego has not been built up for any such purpose. As an heir to love relationships which have been sustained by the urges of the id, it is really constructed of id material and is carried within the personality, charged with the energy of the id urges—at least with the sexual energy of the id urges. So it is much nearer to the id than the ego, which seems paradoxical in many ways.

Again, this is a place for a question which is very often asked: is the superego a faithful image of the parents, or is it a faithful combination of part images of several parent figures? One might be very tempted to say yes, but there is so much evidence against it. For instance, you can find children with lenient, tolerant, loving parents, who, on the basis of their relationship to these parents, have built up a severe, cruel superego. When you watch the child at play and see the guilt feelings he develops, how he punishes himself for small misdeeds, how anxious he is, how much he shows inner conflict, you might feel quite certain that this child has had over-strict parents whom he is imitating; but it is not true. You find children of restrictive, severe, or even cruel parents who have very tolerant, lenient superegos, and you find children of loving, permitting parents who are tortured by their superegos. Where does this difference come from, if the superego is a result of identification with the loved figures outside? In fact, the explanation of this has been found, again, through the study of abnormal personalities and with the confirmation from the study of normal personality. What I have shown you so far is that the superego is built on the fate of the sexual urge of the child— namely, the superego is the heir to the child's love relationship. But what about the fate of the aggressive urges? It is exactly the fate of those urges which allows us to explain the harshness and cruelty of the superego, in the following way. The action of the parents in frustrating the child's wishes, as I tried to explain last time, calls forth a great deal of aggression in the child directed towards the parents; and apart from this evoked aggression, there is also the natural aggression that we consider inborn, which appears in the child at the same time as the sexual instinct, and which is directed towards the parents together with the sexual instinct. But then the question arises of how much of these aggressive feelings the child can actually express towards the parents. There are many hindrances to this expression of aggression. One is that the parents may not like it, may not like the child to express his death wishes, his anger, his rage. Before parents gained all the psychological knowledge which they possess nowadays, the aggression of the child towards the parents was considered to be one of the worst things in a child's behaviour, so it was strictly forbidden. Yet even with permissive parents it is not at all easy for the child to express aggression towards father or mother, because the child has an internal conflict—these are loved people, and if one kills off the people, one loves one misses them afterwards. This sort of primitive reasoning exists in a child, but there is no integration possible early on between an unchanged love and an unchanged hate towards the parents. So there is conflict, and such conflicts lead towards prohibition and repression by the child himself of aggression towards the parents. And now a curious factor emerges. This aggression in the child does not merely disappear but has to be used somewhere, so it is used by the superego and directed inwards, towards the ego of the child. This means that the superego of the child becomes harsh and cruel to the degree to which the aggression has been turned away from the parents. And the fact that loving parents give the child much less opportunity for free outlet of aggression explains some of the paradox I mentioned. The child feels much worse about hating loving parents than about hating unkind ones. So the superegos of these children with loving, permissive parents become very harsh indeed, whereas harsh and cruel parents provoke their children to revolt, and in that revolt much of that aggression becomes conscious and can be directed outwards rather than inwards. Consequently the superegos of such children are very often lenient and permissive. These are complicated factors, but the complications are those of life and are not invented by the analyst.[2]

So now you have the three parts of the personality which concern us. The child of the age I described, as I have represented him to you, now has his id urges, his ego functions, the ego content filled by identifications, and the superego, which consists of the most important of these identifications. So you

---

[2]Nowadays we might say that the child who experiences severe conflict because of his ambivalence to his parents *projects* his unconscious aggressive wishes into threatening fantasy figures, which then become incorporated into his superego.

have here the completed personality of the small child; but, of course, that leaves us with many other factors to discuss.

While the child goes through those processes which build up his full personality, he goes simultaneously through the phases of libidinal development which I described to you when we discussed infantile sexuality. So the behaviour of the child, if you want to understand it now, has to be viewed from two sides. On the one hand, we have to look at the structural side and ask which part of the personality is involved in one or other type of behaviour. Is such behaviour occasioned by the id urges? Is it regulated by the ego or enforced by superego commands? Or is it a mixture of all these? If we had time I would discuss with you the implications this has for education: do we address our educational efforts to one or other of the three parts of the personality? And you can very well characterize educational efforts by the part of personality to which they are directed.

Well, that is one view of looking at the behaviour of the child. The view from the other side is to understand the changes in the child's behaviour by reference to the levels of instinct development through which he passes—namely, the oral, anal, and phallic phases, with the accompanying changes in the aggressive urges. There you will find that it is not too difficult to guess what libidinal stage a child has reached by observing his behaviour in his object relationship. On each stage the relation to the object is a different one. To characterize it very briefly, in the oral phase the relationship of the child to his objects—primarily the mother—is dominated by this oral quality of greed—the child can't get enough, urgency and greed are marked; greed for food, for the presence of the mother, for her fondling, for everything. This means that the possession of the object at that time serves the purpose of satisfying the greed. This is a hard time for the mother, as we all know, but it is not as hard for the mother as is keeping up the relationship in the next stage, the anal one, where it is not greed any longer which dominates the object attachment to the mother, but other qualities. The child in the anal phase equally wants to possess the mother, but for other purposes. He wants to have her, to hold her, we might say to 'squeeze' her, but also to hurt her, to torment her, to handle and be handled by her. The object relationship in the anal phase is a very specific infantile one, which can hardly be mistaken. It is very much dominated by the aggressive instincts, by the idea of giving and taking, which is probably connected with the toilet training that takes place at that time. Above all it is an inconsiderate and—I would say—rather a cruel relationship. The child can't let go of the mother, but when he has her he somehow tortures her. I know this does not sound a very friendly description, but every mother of a young toddler of about two years of age would agree, if she is honest, that she feels tortured, and that there is only one element in the situation which makes this acceptable to her—namely, her great love for that child. But this element of being tortured—and, indeed, the whole relationship, which seems to be what we call a 'sado-masochistic' one—comes easily into the foreground of our awareness when the person who takes care of the toddler is not the mother, with her love for the child, but is a stranger. For the stranger, of course, these feelings of being tortured are not mitigated by the same love for the child, and so a battle with the child develops very easily. That is why we hear so many stories of children of that age having bad nurses, being badly treated, being restrained too much, being punished too much. It needs complete affection for the child in order to bear the difficulties of the love–hate relationship which becomes so obvious in this stage.

And then the child passes on his own from the anal phase to the phallic phase, to the genital level of the boy, and his behaviour changes completely. All the sado-masochistic interplay disappears, and the child, especially the boy (I have not forgotten the girls—they come in a little later), adopts a purely masculine attitude of love, protectiveness, helpfulness towards the mother. This is very pleasing to the mother and a very different experience from what has gone before. It is not education that has changed it, and it is not that the id urges at that time are necessarily under better control than they have been in the anal phase. It is that the aim of the phallic phase, in regard to the object, is a different one. It is not any more to possess and torture the object but to admire and be admired by the object. This is the phase where, for the boy, the wish to impress the mother with his strength, with his skill, with his bodily perfection, with his phallic erections, is uppermost. If you watch the interplay of mother and child in the phallic phase, you will be surprised how often one word returns in the exclamations of the child, and that word is 'Look!' It is a continual demand on the mother to look: look how well I can do this, how I can do that, look at what I have just done. I remember one little girl of seven or eight, who was together with such a boy of three, asking me whether the name of his mother was 'Looky', or something like that—well, it very nearly is. It is a great relief for the mother when this stage is reached, though the child needs her just as much as he has before. With some little boys—and that is again a very curious thing—the love for the mother, this helpfulness for her, this admiration for her, is mixed with a slight contempt—she is only a girl. And little boys express that very often, and some of the helpfulness that they show towards the mother comes from that source. After all, what can the poor girl do, she needs a man to help her. All this is expressed in the attitude of the boy, and it is something about which his feelings are quite serious.

And now the boy has reached the stage (girls have reached this stage as well, but I will describe the boy first) that you have heard referred to in the literature and in your studies as the Oedipus complex. The boy is now man enough to be a full rival of his father and to claim the full possession of the mother in a masculine way. I thought that I would take you today up to the stage of the Oedipus complex in its simplest form and that we would leave the whole next lecture to enter into the complications of it, the abnormalities of it and the variations of it which you find in the development of the girl.

Towards the Oedipus Complex

Quite a number of questions came in last time. Some of these related to the theory, and I don't think I can do much more than name them. There was the almost inevitable question about whether aggression is inborn or whether it is produced by the frustrations which the child has to suffer. The questioner wanted to know whether there was any direct evidence to show that aggression exists without frustration. Well, there is no direct evidence, because those people who would like to prove it are hampered by the fact that there is no such thing as life without frustration, and only if we could have a child who experienced no frustrations could we prove that aggression is there nevertheless. I suppose discussion of these different theories of aggression will accompany you further through your dealings, but you will realize that our theories are formed, not so much on the basis of direct evidence, on the observation of single cases, but, rather, on overall impressions. The theories are tried out to see whether they fit the facts, whether they make it easier to understand the facts. If they do not fulfil that particular purpose for any length of time they are dropped again. Well the theory of aggression being inborn has not yet been dropped—or, I should say, very many people hold on to it while very many other people doubt it, so you can take it as an open question.

The other theoretical point is easier to answer. Somebody wanted to know whether the description, as I gave it last time, of the ego being built up of identifications negates completely the idea that temperament and character can be inherited factors or can contain inherited elements. My answer to that would be that nowhere in psychoanalytic theory will you find the negation of inherited factors. What we always imagine is that there is an interplay between inherited possibilities and reactions to experiences caused by the environment. It is always both sets of factors which contribute to the final result. So that this question can best be answered by saying that the identifications build up the ego on the basis of whatever inherited material there is in the individual; and that applies to the question of inheritance versus experience all through the analytic theory.

One question which showed very good understanding and was, at the same time, really a puzzlement about terminology was whether what I termed 'narcissism', the turning of libido inward towards the ego or towards the body of the child, is identical with the name we use for the various activities which the child performs on his own body for the purpose of gaining pleasure—namely, those activities which lead to self-satisfaction in the oral, anal, and phallic phases. Well, we do not use the same term for both sets of manifestations. By narcissism we refer strictly to the direction taken by the libido, to the use of the libido; whereas we call these other activities auto-erotic, which means erotic activities for which the individual needs no other object except his own body. But the two—narcissism and auto-erotism—overlap somewhere, of course, because it is the inward turning of the libido which, at the same time, has something to do with the erotic feeling produced by the body itself. It is the body which is the source of erotic feeling—we would say in psychoanalytical terms that the body has 'erotic zones'; but the body is also a receptacle for libido, it is narcissistically charged. So that would answer the question.

A further question related to the way the straight line of normal development, which I described deviated into abnormal or peculiar development when there are changes in the environment, where the family setting is not complete, with the result that the child could not build up all three relationships, to father, mother, and siblings; or where there is some inner hindrance to development in the child even though the outer setting is complete. There was also a complaint—which came quite appropriately and which I shall try to deal with today—about feminine development being neglected. There was a further question about the appearance of the object relationships I described in children brought up in those settings where the parents take second place and the community first place, as happens, for instance, in the group upbringing practised now in Israel in the so-called 'kibbutz'—namely, the agricultural community. These are very interesting questions to answer, but they would lead us too far away from our main object. We have every right, of course, if we want to pursue the whole subject more in detail, to go from family upbringing and its consequences to group upbringing and its consequences. I mention these questions to you even though I shall not answer them to show you some of the possible things you might be interested in while following these lectures. You will find that there is ample literature to satisfy your curiosity.

You will remember last time we left the male child in the middle of his phallic development, with that special attitude to the mother and the father which you hear spoken of as 'the Oedipus complex'. The Oedipus complex has become, in recent years, so much a byword, the term has gone over so completely into ordinary language, that few people stop to puzzle out what its implications really are. The simplest way to describe it is to say that the boy has adopted the masculine attitude. His main wish is possession of his mother; his main rival, hindering the fulfilment of that wish, is the father. This means that his love is directed towards the mother, and his death wishes, his hate, is directed towards the father, who is at the same time his love object from earlier times. This creates considerable conflict in him. As you know, this complex situation has received its name from the Greek myth where the hero finds himself in the same situation—namely, having killed his father and marrying his mother. By building up the whole story of the object relationship of the boy step by step last time, gradually and carefully, I wanted you to see in the Oedipus complex something more than a momentary attitude of the child, or something that lasts perhaps half a year and then disappears again. The Oedipus complex is the climax of all the earlier development, and the form it takes in the child is more or less completely determined by what has gone before—namely, by the oral and anal relationship to the mother, by the earlier wishes to get hold of her, to possess her, and by the amount of fulfilment and frustration which the boy has experienced during these earlier stages.

You could say that for the child wanting to have the mother is far from new. It has been there from the beginning, from the first time the child was nursed by the mother, or from the first time the mother, rather than the nourishing breast or the milk, became the child's object. But the child's relationship to the mother in these earlier phases is piecemeal, taking little account of her personality as a whole. The child always wants something, never gives anything, and it is only in the phallic phase that for the first time the relationship takes on an adult form of exchange. There is, of course, one important point about the real aim in the relationship with the mother that differs from the adult aim. While in both cases possession of the woman is the aim, in the boy what is involved is not the idea or the fantasy of intercourse (which, by the way, the boy of that age is incapable of carrying out), but the idea of exhibiting his masculinity to the mother and so to win her admiration for his manhood. It stops at that, though in certain children we can find vague fantasies that go further—fantasies of crashing through a forbidden opening, of entering a forbidden room, and so on; such fantasies definitely foreshadow later intercourse.

This phallic–oedipal phase has more significance for the child than one might think at first glance. When adults recognized it first, and when parents permitted themselves to notice the masculine attitude of the little boy, they used to find it very pleasing, but at the same time humorous; they saw a little boy trying to act as if he were a big man. In fact, the fate of this phase is decisive for the fate of that boy's later masculinity. If something happens in the phallic phase which frightens the boy out of his masculine attitude during the oedipal relationship to the mother or which induces him to retreat from it, he may lose it forever after. Well, how can this come about? The answer is that it comes about mainly in two ways. Due to the rivalry with the father, the boy fears the father's competition. He sees the father as more powerful, stronger, and the father can punish him for it. Here again are vague ideas, which sometimes become quite strongly explicit in the boy's mind, that he will be punished by losing his genital. This means that because his greatest wish is to get admiration for his phallic powers, his greatest fear is that he might lose his penis. If you analyse a boy of that age, you invariably find such fantasies in his unconscious. In many children they break through to consciousness at that time and express themselves quite openly in what we call 'fears of castration'.

Due to these fears, the boy may give up his masculine attitude to the mother and may withdraw from his masculinity and turn back in his development. As we put it, he will 'regress'— namely, his libido will retreat to earlier stages which were safer; the child will go back to a relationship to the mother of the oral or of the anal kind, which seems less dangerous and not so threatened by outside forces. So you will very often see a boy of that age suddenly lose all the promising and pleasing masculine qualities and sink back once more into the attitude of a helpless, tormenting, querulous infant. The same thing may happen for a different reason. The boy may notice that his fantasy attacks on the mother, or his attempts to get the mother to admire the masculinity of his body, actually displease the mother. He may even feel sorry for the mother who is now, we might say, attacked by two men; or he may have noticed her rejecting attitude towards the father's advances to her—this happens in many marriages, where the wife is frigid. The boy may then make up his mind that he would be a better partner for the mother, that he will make no such forbidden demands on her—another reason for him to drop his masculinity and retreat. Or his love for the father may be so great that he cannot bear to be his rival, and again he will retreat; and there is a further reason which we will discuss presently.

Whatever the reason, the boy has open to him a path which leads backwards. And taking it is a major decision (not a conscious decision, it is not that the boy says to himself, 'I'd better not continue in this attitude of mine, I had better behave as I did before, and my mother and father will love me much more'—it doesn't happen that way). The decision is taken as an unconscious automatic response to the danger, to the discomfort which he feels in the situation of the Oedipus complex. And now comes the decisive step, for if he retreats, if he drops his masculine demands, if he becomes more of a baby again, he will enter into the next phase of life—namely, into the latency period, into school age—with his masculinity gone. And when pre-adolescence comes to wake up all that pregenital sexuality again, it will not wake up the reactions of the phallic phase but, above all, those reactions to which the boy turned at the height of the Oedipus complex. This is the reason why many of our male children go through the whole of the important phase of the latency period, of school life, not as proper boys who like to fight and to conquer, to explore and to protect, but as rather passive, rather feminine, complaining, somewhat cowardly children who avoid competition, who do not like to be hurt in any physical way, who are not ready to take risks, and who run to their mothers and complain when anything happens to them. This means that you can determine, even without analysing a child, whether by his manifest behaviour he has been able to retain the qualities of the phallic phase or not.

Perhaps I exaggerated when I said that in the phallic phase and at the height of the Oedipus complex the decision will be made how much of a man this individual will be in later life. This is not completely true. There is, in adolescence, from the biological side, a great surge of genital libido through the personality, and if things go well in spite of the non-phallic leanings that the boy has brought with him, his phallic masculinity can be restored once more. But very often it is only restored for the period of adolescence, when the increase in the genital drive is such a strong one. When adolescence has passed, the regression to the anal or oral phase may reappear. This means that many of the boys who lose the fight for their masculinity in the Oedipal period have great trouble in attaining a normal adult sexuality later in life. That is the reason why analysts have always placed such tremendous importance on the happenings in the Oedipus complex—not because it is so pleasing to find once more the ingredients of a myth that is several thousand years old, but because this phase is the battlefield where the struggle for future adult normality or abnormality is fought out. So I would like you to think of the Oedipus complex of the boy in that sense.

And now, since we are half Radcliffe and half Harvard here, it is high time for the girls who have been, I must say, very patient. They have not done too badly, because in the first two phases of the child's sexual life—in the oral and anal phases—there is really very little difference in the development of the two sexes.[1] Both boys and girls have the mother as their main object of attachment and the father as the second one, both have the same battle with their siblings, and both develop the same forms of aggression as they pass through these early sexual stages; and although there are people who say that the girls are a little less aggressive, I don't think so. For instance, in nursery school, where boys and girls of that age are together and play together, it is very often the girls who have the upper hand. There is not much to choose between the forms of development in those two early stages.

It is, of course, clear where the important differences begin to appear in the phallic stage. According to our analytic findings, both boys and girls enter into that phase with the same expectations, and with the same readiness to have that part of the body which in the boy is the penis and in the girl its corresponding organ—namely, the clitoris—as the centre of sexual feelings. But now all the differences between these two organs arrive on the scene and express themselves in the psychological differences between the sexes at this stage. I mean that the boy has an outside genital to be proud of, to play with, to show off, while the girl lacks that organ and has only the rudiments of it, which prove quite insufficient and very unsatisfactory for carrying the libido and the libidinal manifestations of

---

[1]This has since become a controversial issue.

that stage. The auto-erotic activity at that time is very nearly the same with boys and girls, but is much less satisfactory for the girls than for the boys, owing to the quality and size of the organ. So that the height of masculinity, which the boy experiences, ends, for the girl, in an attempt at something which brings disappointment; and that is the beginning of the change in the girl from boyish manifestations to others which we call feminine ones. And that is not all. There is a second important step which the girl has to make, which the boy is spared. As you will have realized if you have followed my descriptions, the boy keeps his love object in the environment— namely, the mother—constant until adolescence. It is on the person of the mother that he learns to love. She is his first 'whole object', as one calls it, she is the first object in relation to whom he learns the interchange of feelings, and in regard to whom he learns forms of adult love. She accompanies him through the latency period, and when pre-adolescence and adolescence set in, she is still his object. And he has to make an enormous effort in adolescence to detach himself from her and to look for a female object outside the family. It is this detachment which the boy can only accomplish with an enormous amount of hostility against the mother. He has to reject her as a loved person completely before he can get free of her. This is the— often very tragic—struggle between mother and adolescent. The mother cannot understand why her son suddenly turns against her with hostility. There is certainly nothing in her to cause it, or even to respond to it; but the boy can only make a step to an object outside the family if he frees himself from the mother, which he often does in a very brutal way.

The girl has a different fate, as you know, because she has already in the phallic period changed her object—namely, she turned from the mother to the father, and from then on kept the father as a love object. She has the same struggle in adolescence to free herself from him and to transfer her libido to a stranger outside the family, though the struggle is rarely as violent, as harsh—or as tragic, as with the boy. So the girl has two changes to make: one, in relating to her actual physical sexuality, a change in the part of the body which serves sexual pleasure, a change from that rudiment of a male organ, the clitoris, to the feminine organ, which should serve her later in life; and the second change is change of object from mother to father. The boy can keep his genital and does not need to change it, and he can keep to the feminine object. These are the two points from which the further differences in development, in the manifestations of behaviour between the sexes, begin.

Again, I have hardly given you more than the headings for chapters, but you will have no difficulty in finding various essays, papers, books, on female sexuality and its development in the literature, and you will always find these two major changes the girl has to make stressed. You will also find a controversy as to the point in development at which the female genital parts begin to play a role. In recent years there have been authors who, after careful investigation, assert that little girls from early infancy receive certain sensations from their female genitals.

But this is still an open question. Together with it goes another one: are the analysts correct in saying that the wish to be a boy and the disappointment at not being a boy in fact play such a great part in the girl's life? In the theory as I have presented it to you, they do, because, unlike the boy, the girl's fate in later life consists not so much on whether she could keep her sexuality in the phallic phase, but on how she coped with the fact that, after all, she is not constructed for phallic genitality.

This is, then, the normal Oedipus complex, for boys and girls, and you might think it is complicated enough. But it becomes highly complicated by a further factor—namely, that there are no such beings as complete men and complete women. We psychoanalysts believe that there is something basic in human nature that one can call 'bisexuality'—namely, that every male individual has in him the potentiality for female sexuality, and the females have the potentiality for male sexuality in their bodies. And apart from having these potentialities in their bodies, both males and females have them in their mental dispositions. You only need to think back to the question of ego formation as I presented it to you last time—that is, that the content of the ego grows slowly through identifications with the love objects. Well, these are identifications involving both parents. For a long time, for the first two years, boys and girls take their identifications from the mother and build up part of their personality in the mother's image. And when the father comes into the life of the child, the same happens for both sexes in regard to the father. This means that psychologically both sexes carry the rudiments of father and mother, of both sexes, in their mental make-up, in their ego and in their superego. There is a readiness, therefore, in both sexes to react simultaneously as men and as women. This means that every boy, besides having this triangle in his life—the triangle of object relationships in which he loves the mother and is the rival of his father—also experiences the opposite—namely, a triangle in which he plays the mother's part for the father, where the mother is his rival and he offers himself to the father as a love object. We call that the 'inverted Oedipus complex'[2]; and you can imagine now what a powerful addition it is to the regressive forces in the boy, to his need to drop his masculinity and to sink back into earlier phases, and what a powerful addition it is to the feminine side of his nature. For becoming passive once more towards the father, instead of competing with him, corresponds exactly with the feminine side of his nature. So when you find that a boy has regressed from the phallic phase to the anal one, don't be too quick with the diagnosis that he has regressed because he fears his father. He may have done so because the attraction of the feminine side in himself was too great. He could not maintain his masculine position towards the mother and adopted instead the feminine position towards the father.

I was asked a question which I did not answer earlier. The question is whether infantile, adolescent, or adult homosexuality could be the outcome of the experiences of the Oedipus complex. I would like to modify the question somewhat. We do not talk of infantile homosexuality because during the phases of infancy it is quite natural for the child to have a love object of the same sex, just as it is natural for him to have a love object

---

[2]Also known as the 'negative' Oedipus complex.

of the opposite sex. Every boy who has—to use these adult terms now—a heterosexual love for his mother has at the same time a love for his father; and we gain little by calling it homosexual. The same is true in adolescence. Nearly every adolescent passes through a phase where he connects himself with an object of the same sex before he can establish object relationships with an object of the opposite sex. This is partly the repetition of his childhood experiences. For the boy this may represent once more his love for the father. For the girl it may represent again her deep attachment to the mother.

There is another reason why all this reappears in adolescence. Every adolescent goes through a phase when he withdraws from love objects altogether and becomes very egoistic and narcissistic. And when he finds his way back to an object, he usually looks first for an object like himself, and the friend of the same sex then is the bridge to the other sex, for the friend of the same sex represents the adolescent himself, and is at the same time another person. So very many adolescents find their way to the other sex through a short phase of homosexual attachment. We call these attachments 'homosexual' when they persist into adulthood—that is, when the way to the other sex remains blocked and when the individual, on the basis of the inhibitions which he has acquired, on the basis of his inability to leave the objects of the family or to regain his adult masculinity, remains fixed to objects of the same sex. That is, then, what occurs in the adult homosexual, and much has been studied about this abnormality in recent years. At the moment analysts are very much more hopeful than they were ten or twenty years ago, that all these deviations from the norm can be set right again.[3] The inborn bisexuality is, of course, just as

---

[3]At the time these lectures were given, homosexuality was regarded as an illness, which psychoanalysis could hope to cure. The prime aim of analytic work with homosexual patients has changed in the last few decades, for it is no longer the analyst's aim to 'cure' homosexuality as such, but, rather, to analyse the conflicts and fantasies in the homosexual which have led to the request for analytic help, and which re-arise in the analysis—including conflicts over homosexuality.

important in the development of the girl, because it makes it very attractive for the girl to remain longer in the phallic phase than she perhaps should, considering her feminine body and her future fate. One sees little girls in the phallic phase adopt, on the basis of their masculine side, a very masculine attitude towards the mother in rivalry with the father; that is the girl's inverted Oedipus complex.

You have probably read and heard that this phase of the Oedipus complex does not last very long, that it passes. We have already talked about it. But with its passing two things come together, which we ascribe to innate forces in the child. There is a lessening of the id desires at this point, coupled with the frustrations of the Oedipus complex—namely, with the impossibility for boys and girls to realize any of the wishes which belong to the phallic phase. The path to fulfilling them is blocked for both; the rival is there, the fear of the rival is there, and the pull back to earlier phases, as I have described, plays its part. Neither father nor mother is willing to indulge the child as far as these wishes are concerned. This means that under normal circumstances all the desires of the Oedipus complex become frustrated, and this is a very powerful factor in causing them to be dropped, withdrawn, repressed, or having done to them any of a number of other things that can be done with such desires (we will hear more of that later).

If you remember, last time we ascribed an important role for identification to frustrations—namely, these short interruptions in the satisfactory relationship between mother and child. You can judge now what an important role for identification the massive frustration of the Oedipus complex must play; and it really is so. Whatever identifications are made with the parent become enormously enhanced and enlarged in the phallic period and somehow gain independence through this major event in identification. The group of identifications which we summarize under the name of 'superego' becomes more or less completed in that stage. What is added later is negligible compared with what has gone before. This means that the passing of the Oedipus complex and the setting up of an independent superego (namely a superego that no longer connects continually with the environment) come together. Those children who do not pass their Oedipus complex, who get stuck somewhere in the struggle with the parents, fail to gain this final independence of the superego. This means that their superego demands and commands remain attached very much longer than would normally be the case to the environment, to the original objects outside.

It is always dangerous, of course, to use the words 'normal' and 'abnormal', because what I have represented to you as the simple Oedipus complex and its variations is, we could say, always in the range of the normal. Since bisexuality is normal and inevitable, the inverted versions of the Oedipus complex are equally normal and inevitable. Since normal development has so many phases, stages, levels, so many possibilities for instinctive energy to be held back at some place during that long way towards adulthood, there are innumerable possibilities in this normal development to acquire abnormalities. It is really our task to help the parents to guide the child through these phases, and it is an enormous task. It is a problem for all of us to know how much parents can be helped in this by knowing about all these developmental stages, how far that knowledge will help them to lead the child from one stage to the next, or at least to deal with holdups. As you have seen, the possibilities for abnormality lie in two main factors. The gratification of the instincts in each phase may be too satisfactory or too unsatisfactory, and as a result instinctual energy—that is, libido or aggressive energy—will remain fixed to that phase, and whenever a difficulty arises at a higher level, the child will be pulled back to the level of development where such a fixation has taken place. To put it in analytical terms, the great dangers in a child's development are the fixations and the regressions. What we would hope for the child is an orderly progression through all the difficulties that lie on the way, until the final stage of adult instinctual life is reached, both as far as the drives are concerned and as far as the objects on whom these drives should find satisfaction are concerned. It should be possible to delegate the task of guiding the child through these developmental difficulties to the parents and to the teachers. At the moment an enormous amount of help seems to be needed from psychiatrists, analysts, and so on, but perhaps only because parents and teachers have not yet learned enough about these matters.

* * *

We are left with two meetings to show all you future parents in more detail how the child actually handles these dangerous drives, what methods are used to secure smooth development, and what possibilities are open to the environment to influence them.

The ego's anxiety
and its effects

We had better begin again with questions. There were many after last time, and I had to summarize and telescope them into a few. Some were more or less inevitable offshoots of the subject which I would certainly have introduced into the lecture itself if I had not been pressed for time. For instance, several people raised the question of what happens if the family situation is not complete. We speak in relation to normal development as if the presence of the father and mother were inevitable ingredients of the situation, but, of course, we know from clinical and social experience that this is not by any means the case. There are any number of children who have to pass through their phases of development without either father or mother, losing father or mother in the middle of their development or growing up without one parent almost from the beginning. Naturally these situations have been studied and have even contributed most valuable insights to our knowledge of the normal family situations. There is no doubt that aspects of the Oedipus complex change in many ways when there is no father or mother present. Yet at the same time it is surprising to see how much effort the child makes to complete the situation and to acquire for himself the missing parent—or, rather, a substitute for the missing parent—from somewhere else. Illegitimate children, for instance, who grow up with a mother and without a father, do not only feel the social stigma which in many communities still attaches to that situation. The boys in the oedipal phase feel very keenly that there is no father figure on the basis of whom they can mould their beginning masculinity, on the one hand, and with whom they can compete, on the other. Instead of being glad of the opportunity that they have much more free access to the mother than the normal child, they look for father figures everywhere, and, as I have often seen, they greatly embarrass their mothers by offering them all the nice-looking men whom they meet, perhaps on a walk, as a daddy. They urge their mothers towards marriage, to provide themselves with the very object towards whom they will experience rivalry and competition a short time later. This is a very special factor which leads to the question of whether the family situation and the Oedipus complex is in some way prepared for in our children—these attitudes can't be inherited as such, but we don't know whether there is something in the child prepared for them and serving to arouse the oedipal feelings, because they have been repeated in the cultural environment over so many generations. This problem has been approached by many people from many sides. I can give you one observation from my own experience, and that is that when you take children out of a family setting for some reason or other and bring them up in a community, they take a long time to get used to the community surroundings. But when children are brought up in community surroundings and are then placed by adoption into a family, under lucky conditions they take a very short time to acquire the family attitudes, and even the jealousies of the Oedipus complex, as if the family setting were very much more appropriate for their nature than the other. Whoever is interested in such questions will find plenty of opportunity to study the examples of deviations from normal stages given in the literature.

Someone asked under what conditions the superego changes in later life; and the questioner himself names two conditions—namely, that it is well known that the superego can change under the condition of psychoanalytic treatment, and also that it is known that superego demands, and the guilt feelings accompanying them, change after electric shock treatment or insulin coma treatment; and he lumps the two conditions together, which I did not quite like. It is true that in both situations something happens to the equilibrium of the personality, but it happens for very different reasons. If you remember how the superego is built up out of the earliest identifications of the child, then you will understand why psychoanalytic treatment can modify the superego, by leading the individual back to that earliest time of life, by reviving once more the object relationships which gave rise to these identifications, and thereby going to the very root of the identifications underlying them. That is the procedure in psychoanalysis. Whereas in shock treatment, with the resulting changes of personality, something of a very different kind happens, though no one has described its psychological implications fully; but something like a slight (sometimes a graver) depersonalization of the individual happens: the anxieties, the guilt feelings, the wishes, desires, the worries, which were present in that abnormal personality before the shock treatment, do persist, but they become somehow dimmed, they are less important, they are less keenly felt. The change seems to be a quantitative one, and it affects not only the superego, it affects all parts of the personality. So that is a different matter altogether.

Someone asked whether self-love and object love, which means narcissism and object love, are necessarily contrasting; do they not co-exist always? This worried me, rather, in case I had perhaps given you a wrong impression. Of course, they co-exist. There is no such thing as an individual with pure self-love—except perhaps a severe schizophrenic who has withdrawn all love from the outside world[1]; and there is no such thing as a person altogether emptied of self-love, of narcissism,

---

[1]The schizophrenic is narcissistic in a *descriptive* sense. Although he may have turned away from the outside world, the objects represented in his fantasy life and in his delusions are highly invested.

who has placed his whole libidinal energy on the outside world. The two are always side by side, and it is only the relative proportions of the two that change. But there is—and I had no time to mention it earlier—one state in life, and not an abnormal one, at least not a pathological one, which comes very close to an emptying of the personality of all narcissism and changing it all into object love. You probably know what state that is—it is the state of being in love, when all the feelings which a normal individual uses for himself flow over to a specific object in the outside world, the partner with whom one is in love. People at that time feel quite devoid of egoism, of narcissism, of concern for their own personality; it all flows over to the other person. That is why the loss of such a partner is so extremely painful, because it leaves the individual for the moment empty, empty of self-regard, and he has, through a very painful process, to re-cathect himself with love to feel again that he is somebody, even when his partner has deserted him. So this is an abnormal state but not a pathological one.

And now for something else. There was an undertone in some of the questions which sounded to me vaguely resentful, but I must conclude that the resentment is not directed against me, since I am only the person who describes and presents these matters to you, but perhaps a resentment about the complications, the enormous complications of human life. When we hear how extremely difficult it is for a child to pass through the stages of his development, to by-pass all the dangers on the way, not to be held back anywhere, not to be thrown back to earlier stages of development, to maintain his masculinity or to establish femininity, to reach at last that desired aim of adult instinctual life, it is very understandable that people get discouraged. It is also very understandable that many raise the question in themselves of how it could ever be possible for parents to guide their children through this wilderness of drives, wishes, desires, and dangers. Such a task not only demands a knowledge of all these things; it demands from the parents an objectivity which they cannot possess, because these very drives of the child are directed against them. The parent is the desired partner, the parent is at the same time the object of the child's aggression, the parent is the one who has simultaneously or in very quick succession to satisfy and frustrate the child. Under the impact of the child's desires and in his own insecurity, where is the parent's chance of guiding the child? That is the feeling that is very often created when one takes a good look at these matters, but it is also why one sometimes feels inclined, as a lecturer, to present things in a more simplified and a more optimistic manner than I have done. But I do not think that any service is done by such simplifications to those who listen. After all, you need to know the complications of life, because that is the only chance to master them. This takes us to the next question. If the possibility exists for the outside observer and the guide of the child to lead the unfinished human being to their aim—which is a double one, a quantitative and a qualitative one—then what are his tools? Well, to return to why the aim is a quantitative and a qualitative one, the answer is that because, on the one hand, the urgency of drive activity as a whole has to be reduced during the process of growing up and, on the other, the qualitative changes, according to the levels of development, from pregenital sexuality through to adult genital sexuality, have to be achieved. Both aims can only be reached by introducing a great variety of modification of drive activity into the child's life; and it is with this modification of drive activity that the parent is concerned. But what makes the child amenable to the parent's influence? I think that I prepared you for a very thorough understanding of this particular subject when I described the long period of dependency which the human being has to undergo, that long period when satisfaction for the drives, the gaining of wish fulfilment, the acquisition of pleasure and the lowering of tension needs help from the outside world. Through very many years of childhood, and in the first year entirely, the child is an instinctual being, is completely dependent on the parents, on the mother. And it is this key position with regard to drive satisfaction which gives the parent the chance to influence the child.

It is our task now to enquire in detail about these chances to influence the child. And I think you will be very surprised to hear what the best helper of the parents is in this respect; it is the child's ability to develop anxiety. Anxiety has always been considered the worst enemy of man, and it has always been the greatest wish of parents to free their children of anxiety in one way or another, to lower the level of anxiety in them. They have never succeeded, but they have always wanted to succeed. So how can I say that anxiety is so helpful in the development of the child? You know, when we say that parents take so much trouble to try to free their children of anxiety, we say something which is not true if we enquire into it more closely. We only need to remember that parents teach their children to be afraid of certain things, and that this teaching is very solidly continued through the first three, four, five years of the child's life. So the same parents who want to free their children of anxiety have the task of making them fearful where the real dangers of life are concerned. I suppose you realize that young children, even when they are already able to move, have no conception of the real dangers of the world. They don't know that they might kill themselves if they fall from a great height, that they can wound themselves dangerously if they use sharp instruments, that they can burn themselves if they come too near the fire, that they can be seriously harmed if they approach a big animal. They have to be taught all these things. Parents are very proud when their young infants are fearless, but at the same time are very concerned about this because as long as they are fearless, they are exposed to danger. It is an integral part of every child's education that he should learn something about the real dangers which exist around him. So the parents are very careful to show that the fire can cause a burn, that jumping from a great height hurts, and so on. When the child has understood the danger and is afraid of these situations, he has made an important step in his ego development because he is now able to do something about it. But if he is not afraid, he can't do anything about the dangers. So there you would have one very simple instance (you will guess that it is not the one we really have in mind) where fear can be beneficial. Fear of real danger protects the child, because the child acts on the basis of that fear.

But now let us go away from this very simple fear of real danger to the more complicated psychological dangers and the anxieties which the child develops regarding them. There is another danger which does not need to be taught to the child, which is present in him from the very beginning. This is the danger of losing touch with the adults who provide for and care for the child. The infant in the first year feels great anxiety when he does not see the mother, because he might need her at any moment, and she would then not be there to fulfil his wishes. So the situation of the mother's absence makes him very anxious. A little later the infant becomes equally fearful, that he might by some behaviour of his estrange the mother so that she would be cross with him and withdraw her love. Again this would mean that he is exposed to untold deprivation. The infant is equally fearful that if he displeases these powerful adults who, according to his conviction, hold the keys to everything in their hands, who will do something to him, who will revenge themselves on him in some way—that is what we call punishment. And these fears, which are also fears of an outside reality, but which are made very much bigger by the fantasies which centre around them in the child's mind, do not need to be taught. They spring up quite automatically in the child's mind owing to the dependency of the child on the adult world for wish fulfilment.

Here we have a group of fears, then, that I would like you to consider more or less as one. All the dangers which I have described, which threaten the child, do exist in reality. The separation from the mother is actually possible and happens periodically. The anger of the mother is actually possible and also happens periodically. And the withdrawal of the mother's interest from the child is also well within the limits of possibility and, to the child's mind, happens often enough. Even if the mother turns away, even if the mother is busy with another child, it seems to the child that he has lost the mother's love and interest. These are three big dangers which threaten the child from outside reality, and we can add to them the dangers that have nothing to do with the figures of father and mother, but about which the child has to learn gradually. After all, reality for the child is very dangerous, with numerous possibilities of coming to harm.

When I say the child is threatened, I do not really mean the whole organism, because, as you know from our earlier discussions, the id has no possibility of taking notice of such things; you know, too, that the id pursues wish fulfilment without bothering about the dangers that come from outside. The part of the child which is organized and adapted to be sensitive to danger is the ego. That is why the ego has learned everything it can about the external world, and to spy the dangers in the environment and to guide the wish fulfilment of the id urges accordingly. So danger, and the child's sensitivity to it, is a very important matter for him throughout his life. The reaction to sensing danger is anxiety; the child becomes afraid. It does not matter whether the child's fear is appropriate. Usually the fear is not appropriate. The child fears, for instance, a burning fire or a great height much less than he fears the anger of the mother. The anger of the mother seems much more full of terrible possibilities—as if at the next moment she would deprive him of something, perhaps of parts of his body, or would castrate him; this depends on which fantasies are present. So the fear may not be appropriate to the danger present, but it is appropriate to the importance in the mind of the child of that person in the outside world. We group these fears together under the name of 'fears of reality' or 'fears of the environment'. They are a normal occurrence, but you can see what a dangerous power is put into the hands of the parents. The description I gave you last time could easily have raised the expectation that the parents have no power over the child, but that is not true. Because the parents represent such a danger for the child, they have enormous power, and in the past the parents used the child's fear of losing their love and of being punished, to guide the child's actions completely, which is a dangerous procedure. Some of it needs to be done, but if parents use their power to the full, the fears get much increased, and the child's actions are then not guided by the ego any more (even though the ego develops increasing power and sensitivity) but by the direct fear of the parents. So here is one of the sources from which education gets its power. It is very worth while for whoever is very deeply interested in children to watch out for these anxiety reactions in them. There is no doubt that under the impact of the fear of the environment children will modify their behaviour and will even go very far in modifying the drives themselves; but in this connection they may go very much too far, which means, as you will understand later, that they will become too inhibited, too restrained, and too restricted in their activities.

Well, it would be quite enough if there were no other dangers for the child apart from those derived from the parent figures in the environment; but this is only the beginning of it. Now it is worth remembering another part of the lectures—namely, our discussion of the building up of the superego and the identification with the parents. We need to realize that from a certain time on the parent figures do not only lead an existence in the outside world but are represented simultaneously somewhere in the ego, in the part that is then to some extent separated off from the ego—that part we call the superego. And the threat that the parents outside represent is also identified with; so that now there is a rather frightening figure within the child's ego—the superego—and the threatening part of it we call the 'conscience'. It is the function of this conscience in the child continually to hold over the child the threat of this displeasure which the parents had represented as a threat to the child from outside. Only the conscience is very much harder for the child to bear than the fear of the parents; because there is one saving feature in this fear-relation of the child towards the parents. In the absence of the parents, the child feels comparatively free of that fear. The fear of the parents, once it is taken over into the superego, is all the greater because it is not only that the superego criticizes and punishes the child, but it threatens the child for merely thinking certain thoughts. Let us think of a child who, at the oedipal stage, develops death wishes against a parent. The parent will only react if these death wishes are expressed in hostile actions. If the child carries them around quietly in thought, the parent won't react, because he doesn't know them, but to the extent that the child at that time has a functioning superego and conscience, the mere thought will be scrutinized by the conscience and criticized. It is as if the child had carried out his death wish. His conscience makes him feel bad that he can entertain such a wish towards a parent. The child now develops a fear of the superego, of the internalized parents, which is very much worse than the fear of the real parents and is present all the time; and for this fear, for the criticism of the ego by the super-ego, we use the term 'guilt'. When you hear psychoanalysts talk about the guilt feelings of the child, we mean exactly that—that the child has certain wishes stemming from the drives which he may not have carried out at all, but which are noticeable to the superego and criticized by it, so that the ego of the child experiences the fear which we call guilt. So now we have a child who not only has become fearful of the parents but guilty within himself.

The development of guilt, which comes directly from the building up of the superego (and therefore from the relationship to the parents), follows the rule we discussed last time. Its strength is determined on the one hand by the earlier love for the parents, and on the other by the amount of aggression not used against the parents. So guilt feelings can be enormously strong and tormenting, even where the parents have been rather tolerant and permissive in comparison. The control of the child's action has, with the formation of the superego, taken an enormous step forward, because the child's actions are now controlled by the ego in the service of these guilt feelings, whether the parents are present or not, or whether environmental rules are lenient or harsh. Once a conscience has been established, it is the guilt feelings which urge the child towards renunciation or modification of drive satisfaction. The child experiences this alone now, and the parents can take a step back. Of course, many parents make the mistake of not noticing this change in their children and continue to control them, to threaten them, and to guide them when the guidance should have been left long since to the child's conscience.

We have had one anxiety, the so-called fear of reality, and now we have the fear of the superego—namely, guilt. One might think that there was now not much further possibility for drive satisfaction—or at least for free drive satisfaction—but the story goes on. The ego is in a central place in the mind, with an orientation towards three sides. It becomes extremely sensitive to the presence of danger—danger from the outside world, danger from the superego, and danger from a third side to which we now have to turn—namely, danger from the drives themselves. The ego is extremely attentive to the representations of instinctual life which reach the mind; and the ego is, of course, very suspicious of the drives. There are, of course, certain drive activities of which the ego approves and which are then carried through to satisfaction without raising anxiety—in such cases the ego fulfils the original function for which it had been set up as helpmate of the id. But then we come to all those occasions when the ego ceases, on account of its anxieties, to be a helpmate to the id. While sensing the drive activities, at the same time the ego senses what troubles may arise from them. There are certain drives which, as the ego knows, are forbidden by the outside world. If they were to be carried through to satisfaction, the fear of the environment would immediately arise, because the child would endanger himself, would displease somebody, would call down on himself punishment of some kind. So these drive activities represent dangers for the ego. In the pregenital stages the dangers usually arise from the activities which are left over from an earlier stage; in the oedipal stage it is the forbidden oedipal strivings which would bring the child into conflict with father or mother, as well as the death wishes which would deprive the child of his favourite objects if such wishes were permitted to go over into action.

Due to the fear of the id drives the ego takes the position—a rather hostile position—towards drive activity within the personality and develops a very definite fear of the drives, a fear of the id, a fear of the wishes and fantasies (that is, the images) which are present in the id. It is this fear which you commonly hear referred to as 'neurotic anxiety'. For instance, take a particular child—for example, as described in a case history you may know of: Little Hans[2], who had such a fear of horses that he did not dare to go out into the street because he feared that a horse would bite him. You might think, if you were given that case to assess, 'Oh well, that's a child who has learned some-

---

[2]Described by Freud in 1909 in his 'Analysis of a Phobia in a Five-Year-Old Boy' (1909b, *Standard Edition*, *10*).

thing about outside reality. He knows that big animals can be dangerous.' By no means! He is not really afraid of the horses. The horses represent to him something about his own father, and because his oedipal wishes make him so angry with his father, he thinks the father must know all about his anger (that's his conscience saying that one shouldn't have such wishes against the father), and that his father will punish him for it. So he is partly influenced by fear of the father and partly by guilt feelings—namely, by fear of his conscience. These two dangers make him very much afraid of his own wish to have the mother for his own. And then the whole thing may express itself in a symptom, in a phobia which prevents him from going out into the street; in short, in the form of what we call 'an infantile neurosis'. And whenever a child develops neurotic symptoms of this kind, this is always determined by such a fear of the instinctual drives, by what we call 'neurotic anxiety'.

We ought by now to have reached the end of our story—I think that our child is fearful enough. But there is one more reason for the child's anxiety. I have described how powerful the id is and how very small and powerless in comparison the ego is. It borrows its strength from the id drives; and sometimes when there is a sudden increase in id wishes, the ego feels its position is precarious. It becomes afraid of the quantity of the id wishes, of being overwhelmed from inside—in spite of its organization, in spite of its conscience—its guilt feelings—and its sensing the reality of the outside world. It is afraid of being driven into some kind of emotional outburst, of being overrun from within, of producing a temper tantrum, what we might call in the older person an 'outburst of rage', and something which might result, in the adult, in a crime of violence. The fear is that such outbursts might result from a sudden big increase in forbidden drive activity bursting through and overwhelming the ego. So there is a certain type of anxiety in the human being which is related to the strength of the drives and becomes manifest in those times of life when the strength of the id wishes increases for some reason: for example, at the height of the Oedipus complex, at the height of adolescence, and later in life once more, during the male and female climacteric. The anxiety produced is the most sinister kind of anxiety. Those

EIGHT: THE EGO'S ANXIETY AND ITS EFFECTS 117

who are interested can study it in patients who are on the verge of developing a psychotic illness, which represents another form of being overwhelmed from within. You will then find such patients trembling on the verge of losing the intactness of their ego and of being overwhelmed by their id content.

If you now review the whole position, I think you will alter your opinion that there is really no way of influencing the child, that drive activities go their own way with very little chance of being influenced from outside. Rather, you will look at the whole picture, with the opposite picture in your mind—namely, that these drive activities are enormously threatened and can barely survive in the face of the ego's anxieties. And now you will understand perhaps why parents—at least, well-meaning parents—have always tried to make their children less fearful, why it is one of the main ideals of human beings to be without anxiety. I don't know about American folklore, but in European folklore and myth we have several fairy tales of heroes who did not know what anxiety was, and who braved every danger without feeling it. Well this is an ideal state which no one can reach, and, of course, the person who would reach it would have uncontrolled id activity. So it is a tricky business. You know that some parents have made enormous attempts to decrease the fear of reality in the child by reassuring children that they will never withdraw their love from them. They do this irrespective of whether the child is good or naughty; and they will never punish the child in any way that is harmful to the child. They succeeded in this way in making the child less fearful of parent figures and of the outside environment. But do you know what has happened instead? The children began to lack the guidance which the fear of the parents gave to their id and felt more directly exposed to their id urges. So they made up for the decrease in their fear of reality by an increase in id anxiety, of their fear of the id; and then they were just as fearful as before. If you look at those children who are brought up very permissively and progressively, you will notice that they develop just as much anxiety, perhaps at slightly different times and on slightly different occasions. But so far we have not really succeeded in reducing the overall amount of anxiety in the life of the child.

Well all this is a rough picture of what the dangers perceived and the anxieties experienced by the ego do in regard to modification of the drives. Next time I want to describe the methods at the disposal of that individual in danger situations, to consider how the child, under the impact of these fears, come to grips with his drives.

Prohibitions
and permissiveness

I should have liked to have gone further into the very appropriate questions I have received on the subject of defence. I wish we had a few more hours. It is Columbus who deprived us of that possibility.

I know also that I summarized too much and that perhaps I did not convey to you sufficiently the all-important fact that, in spite of the enormous power and relentlessness of the drives, there is a saving quality—namely, that the drives are so eminently modifiable. The methods which are at the disposal of the personality for such modifiability bring about the necessary adaptations to cultural aims, to the demands of society, even though at the same time they may endanger the efficiency of the personality. I would have liked to say very much more about the fact that the modification of drives is, on the one hand, responsible for social health and, on the other, it threatens individual mental health.

Still, there are a few questions which I have to answer. Somebody asked whether a change of superego is possible in later life, for after all this is so important in regard to the whole

119

question of defence, since the ego so often undertakes defence under the command of the superego. That is a good question for you to follow through the literature. If you do so, you will find that after the period of early childhood, after the passing of the Oedipus complex, there is a comparative closing up of the superego. This means the gaining of a certain amount—or a large amount—of independence of the relationship to the object from which the superego was derived. Of course, this independence is never completely gained, and the degree to which the superego remains under the influence of the outside world is at the same time the degree to which the mature individual is still under the influence of the social environment. This can take the form of a fear—which is then directed not towards the superego, but towards the community—namely, 'am I acting right?' 'what will the others say if I act that way?' This is called 'social anxiety'.

Someone asked where the id gets all the power which is used for modifying the drives. The answer is that there is only one source of power—namely, the id—and that even the power used by the ego against the id drives comes (by a complicated process) from the drives themselves.

I was asked: what about projection? Does it only take place after a superego has been formed? This is a question about which people are not yet quite in agreement; which merely means that not enough clinical observations have been made. But I think that all these defence mechanisms are operated by the ego, and so they operate before a superego has become independent; they operate namely under the influence of fear of the environment. This is 'fear of reality', as we call it, really fear of the love objects; or they operate under the influence of internal anxiety. An ego has to be formed, but the superego does not need to be formed so soon.

Someone wants to know whether all the defence mechanisms presuppose the action of repression first, whether it is what repression has not been able to accomplish that is then accomplished by the other defensive methods. That is not quite so. For instance, a reaction formation will always wait until repression has taken place and will then come in afterwards. Sublimation will usually be based on a certain amount of repression having taken place first. But identification and projection, for instance, do not presuppose the method of repression. They can attack the drive or defend against it by direct action.

And then there is one further question: somebody wants to know what really happens in the process of sublimation. Is the object changed, or is the activity changed? Well, in analytic terms we would say what has really changed is the aim of the drive. This sometimes involves a change of object and sometimes involves the modification of the activity and usually involves both. For instance, if you take the aggressive aims of hurting other people, if this aggressive aim becomes sublimated, the activity—the doing of something hurtful to the other person—remains, but the person is usually changed from an all-important person in the family to a less important person outside; and then the activity is modified from hurting to helping. The aim is changed, but the activity remains sufficiently the same so that it provides the individual with a similar kind of pleasure. We see this, for instance, in the smearing activities of the little toddler, which are sublimated in the form of modelling and painting.

I know that these answers are insufficient in themselves, but I wanted to show you the direction the thoughts of people went in after the last lecture. The direction is an excellent one, for it reflects the wish for more intimate and detailed knowledge about these all-important processes. If we want to apply that knowledge, we have to have much more than an overall picture.

And that brings us now to the question of application. I hope that the motive that went into multiplying the audience today was not that you expected me to tell you exactly how parents should treat their children, on the basis of what we know about childhood development. I hope that you do not expect me to give prescriptions: if a child misbehaves, do this; if a child becomes depressed or shows neurotic symptoms, do that; love your children, or don't love them too much. Well, I can give you nothing of that kind. What I want to show you today is a trend, to show you how the psychoanalytic knowledge about childhood development in the last thirty or forty years has been able to influence the handling of children, where these ways have gone wrong, why they have gone wrong, where they have gone right; and how you can help to improve the methods of application of psychoanalytic knowledge for the future. This is a tall order for three quarters of an hour.

Let us take the historical point of view first. Psychoanalysis, as a science, has never set out to be a psychology of childhood. That came about by chance. While digging down into the past of adult neurotic patients, the discovery was made that the origin of all mental illnesses lay in the early years of childhood, and that whenever one followed a neurosis or another kind of mental disturbance back to its beginning, the knowledge that was brought forth was knowledge about the early years of the personality. This knowledge was collected slowly, and the sum total of it gradually created a psychology of childhood. Even now you will not find this knowledge in the textbooks under that title, but you will find the psychoanalytic theory of personality or introductions to psychoanalytic theory. This means that we intend to describe adult behaviour and motivation, but this invariably turns into a psychology of childhood, simply on the basis of the fact that it is the early development of the adult individual which is decisive for his later personality. And in the same manner, psychoanalysts never meant to contribute anything to education in the beginning. It took a very long time before anybody began to bring the systematic application of psychoanalysis to the upbringing of children. The so-called 'psychoanalytic' educational system (or whatever you want to call it—it is certainly no system yet) is a by-product of psychoanalysis, a by-product which came about in a most unsystematic—and you might say unscientific—manner. The first people who learned about the facts I have presented to you first were the early analysts and their patients. Then gradually there came the students who had been introduced to the same discipline and therapeutic method; and all these people had children of their own. So when these people saw and understood how the handling of children in the early years can produce considerable damage for all of later life, they became afraid that they could perhaps, inadvertently, do the same damage to their own children. As a result, whenever they learned about some new factor in the development of the personality and how it was influenced by handling by the parents, they quickly translated it into actions towards their own children. This means that the first psychoanalytic educators were the analysts and their patients, and it took some twenty years or more until the world of teachers became interested in the same matters. If you think over the material which we discussed in these last meetings, you might be struck by those points which seem of special importance for the handling of children. I wonder whether, as parents, you might have picked up these points on your own.

I shall try to give you something of the history of the way this knowledge slowly filtered through into the nurseries. Before psychoanalysis, people had not known that children had a sexual life, and they had taken as completely harmless the emotional life that goes on between parents and child—I mean the fondling, the expressions of affection children show to their parents and parents to their children. So when there was the discovery that there is something like an infantile sexual life which can be stimulated from the side of the parents and which the child tries to live out on the parents, the expressions of the child's love and affection suddenly took on a very different character. Many people began to be afraid that by kissing and fondling their children, by responding to the advances which they now recognized as sexual advances, they were perhaps seducing their own children. They were especially afraid in view of the fact that in the analysis of adult patients the fantasy of being seduced by one of the parents always used to play a part. Since children have these fantasies—I recall to your mind those of the oedipal phase that I presented to you in some detail—it would, of course, be easy for parents to play in to it, raising hopes in the child (namely, seducing the child)—hopes that cannot then be fulfilled; and this would mean frustrating the child all the more. It was also easy to do what in fact parents used to do—namely, to make light of these advances of the child, to find them amusing, cute, to laugh about them, thereby hurting the child's feelings very much. So the first impression gained by parents from psychoanalysis was that here was dangerous material in the child—infantile sexual life—which needed more careful handling than they had thought necessary before.

Now a further point. In the analysis of many adults it was shown that observations by the child made of the parents at night was a powerful incentive to the child's sexual fantasies, because in those times it was the habit to have young children sleep in the same room with their parents. Parents thought, 'well, children don't notice, they don't see anything, and if they do notice they don't understand'. It became apparent through psychoanalytic investigation that children do actually understand, and that witnessing the parents' sexual life can be harmful to them by provoking responses and reactions from them which are too powerful for their young age. So an important application of psychoanalytic knowledge to the handling of children became the rule that children should not share their parents' bedroom and should not witness their parents' intercourse. All this came about very gradually.

The stages of sexual development, which people began to take notice of next, changed the handling of children enormously. You know, thumb-sucking, dirtiness, masturbation, childish curiosity, childish exhibitionism—showing off in front of the parents—had all been known before, but they had been regarded as 'naughtiness' of children, the 'bad habits' of children. Parents had always wondered where these bad habits came from. They always complained that no sooner had one bad habit disappeared than another one began—which is a very nice description of the orderly sequence of infantile sexual development. Then they realized that these were not bad habits which could be held in check by watching the child more closely, perhaps by excluding him from the company of other children who had similar bad habits. They realized that they were faced with something basic in the child's nature, something inevitable, and that they had to respect the sequence. This created an enormous uncertainty, for parents had previously been certain they were acting correctly if they opposed all these trends in the children. This point was expressed quite directly in relation to the subject of phallic masturbation in children, something which had been one of the main points of battle between adults and children in former years. The child's urge to masturbate and thereby to find a bodily outlet for the libido dammed up in his fantasies had been fought and opposed by adults through the centuries. Now it suddenly seemed, as a result of psychoanalytic teaching, that this was perhaps much more normal and healthy for the child than the damming up of the libido without outlet; something which, in the knowledge of analytic practitioners, led to so much symptom formation. So this again led to doubts and insecurity on the part of the parents. Was phallic masturbation a healthy, a normal process in the child? On the other hand, if they did not oppose it in their children, if auto-erotic habits were permitted, would the child not withdraw too much within himself? And would this degree of satisfying himself not make him less amenable to influence from the parents? There are evidently two trends going against each other here, and both can be supported by analytic evidence. On the one hand, we can see the difficulties which arise when an individual withdraws from the environment and supplies his own needs—in this case satisfies his own sexual needs on his own body. On the other hand, problems arise when an individual satisfies himself too easily and is therefore not forced to come to terms with the forces in the environment, with the objects in the environment from whom he should claim satisfaction.

Now this is where the very tricky problems begin. Great hopes were raised in the parents at this time (I am speaking of perhaps thirty years in the past). Sexual curiosity was recognized as a necessary and normal item in a child's life, and the parents now found themselves quite ready to satisfy the child's curiosity after knowing this (I am still speaking of the analytic parents or their patients). The withholding of sexual knowledge, the insincerity of the parents in that respect, the child's unsatisfied wish to know had always created bad feelings between parents and children. Children had so often retaliated by lying to the parents, since the parents lied to them about sex. So that was the era when the important question of sexual enlightenment began to play a role. You will find an enormous literature dealing with how to enlighten children, with how much to tell them about the so-called facts of life, with whether to wait for their questions or to meet the questions half-way, whether to wait for the birth of a new baby before the process of birth is explained, when to explain the difference between the sexes, and so on. Innumerable attempts were made at that time to give advice to parents in regard to all these questions, and very much was hoped from these measures. It had been seen so often that the repression of childhood sexual curiosity led to a general repression and inhibition of curiosity; so that the children who were refused sexual information sometimes became stupid and uninterested children, as if they expressed by their attitude: 'Well, if you don't want me to know that, then I don't need to know anything.' The inhibitions of many schoolchildren could be shown to have arisen from just this conflict with infantile sexual curiosity.

After these attempts at sexual enlightenment of children had lasted ten or fifteen years, perhaps even a little longer, the first disappointments began to show up. It was perfectly true that on the basis of sexual enlightenment much misunderstanding between parents and children, as well as much inhibition of intelligence, were avoided. Before that, one always used to wonder why children under five were so clever and schoolchildren were comparatively so stupid. Of course, the crucial point was the repression of their sexual curiosity. But a tremendous disappointment was waiting for parents in connection with this—namely, that the children did not really expect the enlightenment that they were given. Most of them listen quite respectfully if they are told where babies come from, what the differences between the sexes are, how babies are born, and even how babies are produced—how they get into the mother. But after a short time—sometimes after a few hours, sometimes after a few days—this piece of good sexual information changes in the mind of the child, and if the child gives evidence of his knowledge afterwards, he gives evidence of curious distortions of it. He continues to insist, for instance, that babies are conceived through the mouth and that they are born like excrement; or through the mother's stomach, which is cut open; or that really all children are born as boys, but some of them then have something cut off, and these poor boys become girls; and they have similar distorted pictures of sexual processes. Above all, they have the picture that what father and mother do with each other at night is a violent quarrel in which either the father hurts the mother or the other way around. And it was seen that no sexual enlightenment could do away with these distortions in the child's mind.

When this experience was re-examined and analysed, it led to more interesting knowledge—namely, that these distortions by the child are not arbitrary ones and have nothing to do with the child's level of intellect not yet being appropriate to receive sexual information. Rather, it was found that the distortions are fantasies of great importance to the child and closely connected with the levels of sexual development. So the child for whom the oral stage of development is the most important will have the fantasy that babies are either conceived or born through the mouth. In the violent anal stage children will be quite convinced that it is the violence, the quarrels, the hurting which produces the baby, and the cutting open which is the process of birth. This means that these birth fantasies, these sexual fantasies of children, reflect the level of sexual interest which they have at a certain stage, and all they can do is to translate the objective knowledge they receive from their parents into the language of their own stage of sexual development.

So do not be disappointed if this enlightenment of children does not lead to their having good intellectual information. Parents have to give this enlightenment to their children, and it is interesting for them to watch what the child does with it. Nevertheless, the readiness of the parents to be sincere and open in this respect does something favourable to the relationship between adult and child. It may be interesting for you to remember that in all the fairy tales which reflect the child's state of mind, the birth processes are represented, for instance, by the queen who wants a baby always eating something to produce that baby. Many other details of childhood sexual theories appear in the fairy stories too.

I did not have time last time to dwell on the defence mechanism which the child uses in regard to his anal urges, to his love for dirt and his interest in excrement. The attitudes of the parents with which the child identifies bring about certain qualities in the child which are beneficial, for instance, great cleanliness and disgust with dirty matter—necessary for social purposes to a certain extent. But the attitudes of the parents also act as very restrictive influences on the personality of the child; and where they are overdone, they produce what we call the 'compulsive' features in a child's nature. The knowledge of those changes in the child's personality due to strict toilet training, resulting in a shock-like repression of the anal urges, has brought about the changes in attitudes to toilet training, of which you have certainly heard. Parents now train their children for cleanliness very much later than they used to do, so as to give the childish personality more scope for development before the restrictive tendencies set in as a result of the prohibitions put on the satisfaction of the anal drives. You have probably heard people speak about the disappointment the infant experiences when he is not fed just when he wants to be, when he has to suffer states of hunger in his first year because he lives according to a strict feeding schedule, and you will have heard that these states are rather dangerous in that they may later produce loss of appetite and feeding disturbances. Well when this analytic knowledge percolated through, it led to the feeding of infants 'on demand' in the fear that feeding on a strict schedule might bring about all sorts of unfavourable results. I won't go into further detail, as I think you must have seen the trend. Perhaps you have seen a little more than the trend—namely, how, point by point, the knowledge of bad outcomes, of neurotic outcomes in the adult personality, led to a loosening up of the demands, the restrictions, the prohibitions which parents had formerly made in relation to their children.

What I have described was the first stage of the so-called 'analytic child upbringing', and this stage suffered from several big defects. I think you can see that its orientation and motivation was a very narrow one—that is, the fear of producing neurotic adults. The idea was that by placing too many restrictions on the infantile drives you produce neurotic adults. When parents became aware of that, they said, 'all right, then we'll put no restrictions on our children'. But they disregarded the fact that neuroses are not the only form of mental disturbance in adult life, and that there are other disturbances which are quite definitely connected with too little modification of the drives, rather than with too much. Many children grow up in an environment where, owing to the nature of the parents or to the absence of parents, they are not forced to modify their pregenital drives to any great extent, and as a result very often grow up into dissocial or asocial human beings. So we have two extremes here, and it is no good to be led in one's actions by one extreme only. So I would not think that it is right to have, as an orientation for the application of psychoanalytic knowledge to the upbringing of children, the fear of either neurosis or of some other kind of mental disturbance such as criminality or anti-social tendencies.

A very much better motivation would be provided by looking at the personality as a whole and by aiming at something which we might call an 'equilibrium' between the different parts of the personality, helping the child to create a state of inner harmony. The first shock brought about by psychoanalytic insights certainly did not create an inner harmonious state. I am sure that many of you might say you know why this first stage of analytic education did not work: because the pieces of knowledge which were applied to childhood upbringing were all of one sort. They were all knowledge about the instinctive side of the child's life. But what about the knowledge, which came a little later, of the other side—of ego development, for instance? It cannot be the task of the parents to look after the drives of the child only, and to see to it that not too much drive activity is lost during the process of upbringing. The task of the parents is equally to care for the child's ego and to see that during the process of development the ego gains sufficient power itself to deal with the drives. I can give you examples of where the understanding of the parents had great gaps—in favouring their children's drives by giving satisfaction in the oral stage through feeding on demand; by not training the child early for cleanliness (which meant letting him be dirty and wet until two and a half or even longer); by permitting masturbation, so that the libido would not be dammed up; by permitting the child to be aggressive, so that the superego would not become too harsh. The same parents forgot that while the child goes through the different stages of his instinct development, he has also to make the all-important step from the pleasure principle to the domination of action by the ego in regard to reality—to what we call 'the reality principle'. Children who are brought up in a very permissive manner with first consideration being given to their drive activity learn to live according to the pleasure principle— the search for pleasure and the avoidance of pain and frustration—much longer than they have any right to do. Between the ages of two and five the control of action should go over from the id, which only thinks of wish fulfilment, to the ego, which acts according to considerations of reality. During that time, as you know, the child has to learn to wait for satisfaction, to control his own drive activity, to interpose thought between the wish and its fulfilment, and cannot learn that on the basis of unrestricted drive satisfaction.

So now we have the second important piece of information that has to be added to the first step in explaining to the parents how important the instinctual life of the child is for his future. Now one has, in addition, to explain to the parents how important for the child's future will be ego control of his drives. And if parents do not want to bring up neurotics and inconsiderate primitives, they have to consider both sides, which means they have to take the risk of frustrating the child on ever so many occasions for the sake of building up his ego strength; because ego strength is acquired when the ego has to deal with frustrations. Many parents hesitate to do that because they fear that the child will cease to love them if they frustrate his all-important wishes. Or they may hesitate in case the child will cease to identify with them—after all, parents now know that ego content is made of identifications (although they don't know it in quite that way) and that the superego is built up on the basis of identification with the parents. But the parents should know that unrestricted wish fulfilment is not the best atmosphere in which identifications are made, and that many of the most important identifications with the parents are made at moments when the child is frustrated, when the child withdraws libido from the parents and builds up his own ego and superego on these experiences of frustration. If parents learn to consider both sides of the human personality, and if they learn to work for an equilibrium between the different parts of the personality, their behaviour will, we hope, take on a very different nature. They will no longer be content with an overall attitude of, for instance, permissiveness to the drives instead of the overall attitude of intolerance towards the child's drives. Both attitudes are equally detrimental to the child.

Even from these very summary lectures, you will, I hope, have gained the impression that the fate of the various separate components of the drives is so very different for each component in later life. This means that each drive should be looked at and treated on its merits. As a concrete example, think of the child's oral desires. Is there really a need for the child to repress his oral desires fully? Well, there is not. There is so much opportunity in later life to satisfy these desires in a sublimated form, in a displaced form. It is not only that these oral drives contribute quite legitimately to adult sexuality: in displaced form they can find further satisfaction in the pleasures of eating, in the pleasure of smoking, in the pleasure of drinking (to a limited extent!). This means that a stand made against these oral pleasures (as, for instance, when parents used to fight against the child's thumb-sucking) seems quite unnecessary, because even when these drives are treated very leniently, they need not be a serious hindrance later in life. It is quite different with the anal drives. There is very little room, if any, for the anal drives in adult life. So they demand a great amount of modification from the individual and consequently require a different attitude from the parents to lead the child's ego to modify them. There is no room in adult life for the pleasure in dirt, for the interest in excrement, in the anus. This means that these drives really belong to those partial drives which, in their modifications, contribute largely to the building up of personality. On the other hand, wouldn't it be a great pity to induce the child in the phallic phase to repress his curiosity, as parents used to do? A grown individual without curiosity is such a very sad figure. Curiosity, if deflected from the sexual problems, becomes one of the greatest assets of the child all through childhood. Similarly, the severe repression of exhibitionism in a child's life is such a pity. It is these children who can't perform in school afterwards, who become shy whenever they have to make a public appearance, who have no pleasure in shining in any way before others, who very often lose every pleasure in their bodily appearance. So parents should be careful how they handle that particular drive, because if it is displaced rather than repressed, it can contribute so much to the happiness of the personality.

On the other hand, what about aggression? The handling of aggression in the child on the part of the parent will largely depend on the community into which the child is meant to go. If you want to induce a child to grow into a considerate, gentle, accommodating, appeasing member of the community, don't let him be too free in his aggression in childhood; but if you want him to be courageous and hearty and outgoing, don't expect him to do away with the aggressive drive early in life. Which means, when you are faced with each drive activity separately, don't think of it merely as general drive activity, but think, rather, of each individual component and its later fate in life. As a result you can establish through your handling a relationship between the child's attitude towards it and the later presence or absence of that particular quality, activity, or attitude in adult life.

The advice we can give to parents is therefore not to treat the drives in a quantitative manner, with an overall attitude towards them ('I'm very permissive towards my children'), but in a qualitative manner, looking at the various trends shown by the child and trying to fit them into the picture of an adult; which is a completely different attitude. Why teach nakedness to children who are later supposed to be decently clothed? Perhaps the result is that you raise the child's expectations of a later free exhibitionism which cannot be fulfilled. But, on the other hand, why take away the pleasure in that trend altogether?

I think you realize by now that if you want to handle these situations intelligently, the way will depend not on vague knowledge of these matters but on your detailed knowledge. This was really one of my misgivings about this course—that I would not be able to equip you with the knowledge which you as future parents will need. All I could do would be to show you the direction in which you can find the knowledge. I would sum it up as follows: what you should have learned from this overall, shortened, abbreviated, summarized, amputated picture of analytic child psychology should give you at least one impression—namely, that conflicts in the human being and in the child are inevitable; they are expressions of the structure of the personality. Do not aim at having a child without conflict, do not aim to spare the child conflict. Equally, frustrations are inevitable. Wish fulfilment on demand does not lead to a development from the pleasure principle to the reality principle, something which distinguishes human beings from animals. What a study of the defence mechanisms should show you is that it is not the absence and presence of conflict, but, rather, the ways and means used to solve the conflict between the ego parts of the personality and the id parts—the drives; and that it is the choice of solutions which decides the normality or the abnormality of the future adult.

* * *

And that is the end of our course.

INDEX